Unraveling the CoVid Con

*The 2020-2022 Blog Posts
of Ken McCarthy*

-

*How One Marketer
Exposed The Truth When It Mattered*

Ken McCarthy

KenMcCarthy.com

Medical Disclaimer
It is not the intention of any of the authors of this publication to offer medical advice. If you believe you need the services of a licensed health care practitioner, please seek one out.

Printed in the United States of America.

1st Edition

UNRAVELING
THE COVID CON

Ken McCarthy

1st Edition

Foreword

You're about to read a real-time, first hand account of the madness that occured - beginning in 2020 - related to COVID-19 (or "The CoVid Con," as it's referred to throughout this book.)

What makes this account so special? The dates these articles were published and how early its author was to identify both the content of the fraud and the methods by which it was being disseminated.

In the very earliest days of the news media-induced CoVid panic, Ken McCarthy interrupted his normal business of advising small businesses, clinicians and non-profits, and focused on pointing out what he believed were obvious holes in the scientific, medical, legal, and logical justifications given by governments around the world for the lockdowns and all the oppressive measures associated with them.

Each one of these posts was time-stamped with the day they were published.

You can visit the blog where these original articles were posted at KenMcCarthy.com

There you will find additional articles that didn't make it into this book along with photos and videos, many produced by Ken himself, including the feature length documentary "Fauci's First Fraud" released in August of 2020 which catalogues Anthony Fauci's forty-plus year career of fraud and corruption.

Together, this book and the blog where these articles were first published demonstrate what rationality, independent thought, and courage looks like in print - and prove that it was knowable from the very beginning that the lockdowns, and all the social and financial harm they caused, were entirely unnecessary and had no rational basis.

This is not the first time Ken has gone on the record with unpopular perspectives.

Before the invasion of Iraq, when the news media and most Americans were cheering the venture, he predicted the occupation would end up "worse than 1,000 Belfasts." In terms of death and economic damage, it actually ended up much worse.

In 1997, he produced the first detailed, comprehensive account of the mechanisms of election fraud in the US, pointing out that both Republicans and Democrats were routinely involved in the crime. Interestingly, his writings on this subject happened to be one of the first blogs. Brassscheck.com/stadium.

On the business side of things, his writings on the potential of Internet video, which was started in 2005 (years before the term "YouTuber" had been coined) were some of the most prescient writings on technology and society in the Internet era. They can be found – time-stamped - at SystemVideoBlog.com

Going further back to 1994, his predictions about the course of the Internet's likely commercial evolution - when few, including Bill Gates and Steve Jobs, could imagine any commercial potential for the web at all - may be the single most insightful talk on the subject in the early years of the medium. You can view the video of that historic talk by searching "When the commercial web was born" on Youtube.

- Paul Morrison

Unraveling The CoVid Con

Table of Contents

Chapter 3. Second Thought: Lockdowns Indefinitely

Chapter 1

The Chinese Scare Goes Global

Coronavirus, stock market meltdown and you

March 09, 2020

Quite a day, isn't it?

Some things you can always count on:

1. Our government and news media will be useless

The only thing the government gets really organized around is selling you out to the highest bidder and coming up with new ways to penalize you for not toeing their line.

The news media can be counted on to get the facts wrong not-so-coincidentally always in favor of their biggest advertisers and government friends.

2. We're on our own

Leaving things that really matter up to "the experts" rarely has a good outcome.

Bottom line: If you're healthy, you have very, very little to fear. However, if there are people in your life you care about who are not healthy, they need extra-special protection and it's not too early to get started.

Financial markets facts

The financial markets have been in meltdown since the summer of 2019.

The little bit of last minute froth in January and February was just that: froth.

Guaranteed your financial planner didn't let you in on the secret.

The only rational thing to do starting around August/September 2019 was to start to buy Treasuries.

Everyone who knows me – or follows my tweets – knows that's what I've been telling everyone who'd listen. VERY few did.

If you've been "financialized" by CNBC and/or a professional financial planner ("you need to be in stocks"), let today be your wake up call.

The financial markets move in cycles.

Stock are NOT always the thing to be in and any "planner" that tells you that you should always be long and overweight in stock index funds should be thrown head first from a tall building.

Bottom line: If you don't know what part of the cycle the financial markets are in, the markets will make mincemeat of you.

The news you're not getting

April 17, 2020

Beginning on March 9, I started writing articles about the shutdown.

Some of these articles contain business advice.

Others are commentaries on what I believe will eventually be revealed as the biggest news media-fueled mass delusion in the nation's history.

…Not unlike what Charles Mackay wrote about in his classic book "Extraordinary Popular Delusions and the Madness of Crowds."

However, unlike Mackay, I don't lay the blame for this social and economic disaster on the public. That belongs to the news media, the politicians and the fuzzy-minded thinkers who believe and echo them without questioning.

Encouragingly, many of the people I talk with have a healthy skepticism about what we're being told. What they don't necessarily have is the time to dig deep into all the inaccurate and fear-provoking claims the news media and politicians are making.

I've also been posting short items to Twitter as I find bits and pieces of important information that the news media carefully leaves out of their evening broadcast of "CoVid-19

Theater." Articles and some highlights of the Twitter posts follow below:

Ken McCarthy @KenMcCarthy · Apr 16, 2020   ···
Italy: 3.18 hospital beds per 1000. Korea has 12.27 per 1000. Yes, hospital systems that run on hair-thin margins have a great deal to worry about in a bad viral respiratory disease season. Note: US holding up the rear at 2.77 per 1000. How does the "news" miss this simple fact?

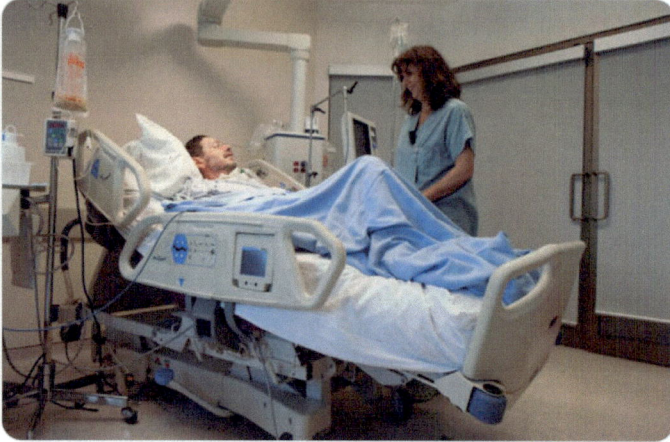

💬   🔁 2   ♡ 3   ⬆️

Ken McCarthy @KenMcCarthy · Apr 15, 2020   ···
Fauci loves pandemics and vaccines and if he has to make up the facts along the way, so be it. Here he is **shilling** for an AIDS vaccine in 2009. He is a master of the Long Medical Con.

> 📄 youtube.com
> More Perspective - HIV Vaccine Shows Promise
> Interview with Dr. Anthony Fauci of National
> Institute of Allergy & Infectious Diseases ...

💬   🔁   ♡ 1   ⬆️

18

Ken McCarthy
@KenMcCarthy

People in nursing homes make up about 0.5% of the population but make up 40% + deaths from CoVid-19. Rather than raise standards for caring for this segment of the population, we demolished 50% of the economy plunging countless millions into poverty overnight.

3:55 PM · Apr 15, 2020 · Twitter Web App

Ken McCarthy
@KenMcCarthy

It's time to end the Epidemiology Amateur Hour
The numbers are in: "Irrespective of whether the country quarantined like Israel, or went about business as usual like Sweden, coronavirus peaked and subsided in the exact same way"
townhall.com/columnists/mar...

11:34 AM · Apr 15, 2020 · Twitter Web App

Ken McCarthy
@KenMcCarthy

···

Governors: "We are getting our advice from state epidemiologists and public health officials." ...In other words, the banner carriers for mediocrity and political careerism are running the world now.

7:45 AM · Apr 15, 2020 · Twitter Web App

Ken McCarthy
@KenMcCarthy

···

URGENT: They're cooking the books on CoVid-19 numbers AND governors are making "shut down" decisions without consulting doctors, epidemiologists or state reps.
youtube.com/watch?v=lsRay1...

9:29 PM · Apr 14, 2020 · Twitter Web App

Ken McCarthy
@KenMcCarthy

···

Make no mistake. This ER/Critical Care physician is risking his job and career by suggesting that CoVid is being treated incorrectly and the "cure" is actually killing the patients.
youtube.com/watch?v=k9GYTc...

3:29 PM · Apr 14, 2020 · Twitter Web App

Ken McCarthy
@KenMcCarthy

···

"Medicare pays $13,000 for a COVID-19 hospital admission For a patient on a ventilator you get $39,000. Nobody can tell me after 35 years in medicine that sometimes those kinds of things impact on what we do." Scott Jensen MD - Minnesota

10:00 AM · Apr 14, 2020 · Twitter Web App

Ken McCarthy @KenMcCarthy · Apr 14, 2020 ···
By edict of **Emperor Cuomo** of New York, the planting of trees is
considering a "non-essential activity. " Not to be outdone, the sale (and I
imagine possession) of seeds to grow a vegetable garden is banned by
Empress Gretchen Whitmer of Michigan. I kid you not folks.

Ken McCarthy
@KenMcCarthy

Saw this last night. Worth a repeat for people who
missed it. Let it sink in. 1/3 of a trillion gone in an eye
blink. Missing from the headline: barely any small
businesses helped. Big publicly traded companies first
in line calling themselves "small" - and getting away
with it.

🌐 **Danielle DiMartino Booth** ✓ @DiMartinoBooth · Apr 16
(Bloomberg) --Funding for a $349 billion federal relief program meant to help U.S.
small businesses survive the coronavirus outbreak has run out, with many still
waiting to get a lifeline, according to an official familiar with the situation.

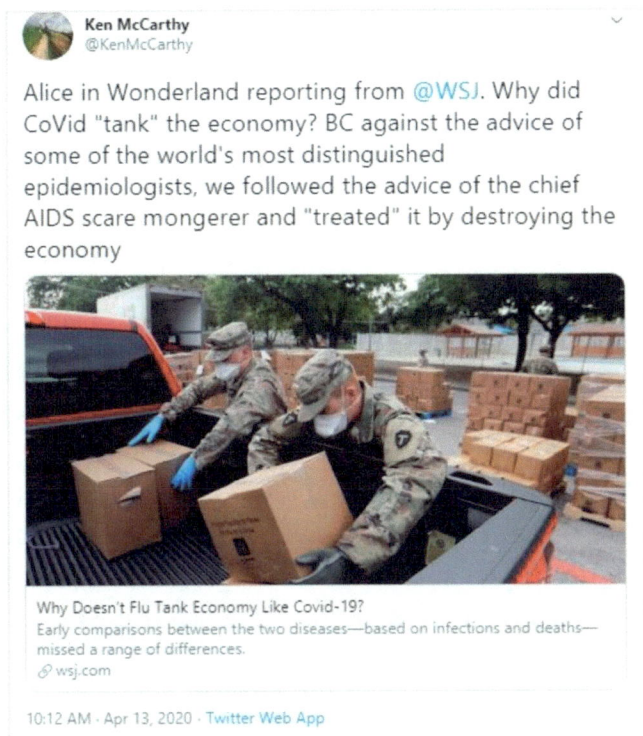

Ken McCarthy
@KenMcCarthy

Alice in Wonderland reporting from @WSJ. Why did CoVid "tank" the economy? BC against the advice of some of the world's most distinguished epidemiologists, we followed the advice of the chief AIDS scare mongerer and "treated" it by destroying the economy

Why Doesn't Flu Tank Economy Like Covid-19?
Early comparisons between the two diseases—based on infections and deaths—missed a range of differences.
🔗 wsj.com

10:12 AM · Apr 13, 2020 · Twitter Web App

So what do we do about all this?

What I said in my March 26th podcast ("What to do now") still applies 100%.

I also provide members of the System Club a steady stream of actionable advice on how to navigate through this mess that none of us created, but all of us are going to have to pay for.

As always, for those who keep their wits, there will be opportunities, and I hope my articles and tweets have helped you keep yours.

Call it "The Shutdown" not "The Pandemic"

April 19, 2020

Words matter and things generally have only one name.

We need to start thinking about how to talk about what's going on. The news media is going to hammer us endlessly with "The Pandemic." I'm going to suggest we start talking about what's happening as "The Shutdown."

Pandemics are a fact of human life.

Their impact ranges from inconvenient to disruptive and, for those directly affected and their families, tragic.

The news media, which has operated as a Hysteria Generating Machine 24/7/365, has put out a great deal of heat, but very little light. The government has jumped on board the bandwagon.

If either of these institutions really cared about public health, there would be hourly public service announcements (PSAs) on TV offering productive and non-hysterical advice, like reminders and tutorials on how to wash hands properly with soap and water and specific details on how to provide protection for family and community members with known risks for negative outcomes.

But we see almost none of that.

Instead it's "all fear, all the time."

Here's the advice the British public health service gave during a particularly nasty flu season in 1949.

"There's a lot of influenza about at present. If you catch it, don't spread it to others"

Simple, clear, practical, useful, and actionable. (No doubt the recent memory of being bombed nightly and shot at helped them put things into perspective.)

We need calm advice like this, but we're not getting much of it.

Instead, we're getting an endless drumbeat of terror: Video of the worst cases run on an endless loop. Projections of total catastrophe based on data that honest medical scientists admit is poor at best. And, sometimes, outrageous and outright misrepresentation of facts.

The theme is: "The government and its public health bureaucracy (which pointedly excludes the input of independent experts from places like Stanford and Yale) knows best and we have to wait for a cure or a vaccine before we can make another move".

Which leads us to "The Shutdown."

Names are definitions and we generally can only keep one definition in our mind for a thing at a time.

The hysteria brigade wants to talk about "The Pandemic" and indeed it's doing so.

What they don't want to talk about – and don't want you to talk about – is "The Shutdown" and its consequences.

I'm surprised at how many people, even some otherwise very sophisticated financial people, are assuming "The Shutdown" is something we'll just have to endure for as long as "The Pandemic" dictates, and that when it's finally over – whenever that may be – we'll all just lick our financial wounds and get back to business.

This is myopic in the extreme.

Let's look at just one thread of the impact of "The Shutdown."

The ripple effect of closing the restaurant industry.

10% of all American workers work in the restaurant industry and we've just destroyed their employers, some of them forever.

Beyond that huge number, there's a whole industry that is based on distributing food to restaurants. They're shut down too.

They're sitting on tons of inventory, some of it perishable, that they have no established channel to sell through. At some point, after they get rid of what they're sitting on, they're going to have to make the decision about re-ordering from their suppliers.

What would you do?

You just got left holding the bag with a mountain of inventory that you now have to write off and you still don't know when your customers, the restaurants, will be able to re-open. But that's not all, when they eventually do re-open – and you don't know when – what will their demand be?

With massive unemployment, which won't be resolved in a minute, and the general panic created around the pandemic, what do you project the demand for restaurant meals will be?

Answer: No one knows.

Some food distributors are going to act defensively and order less.

Food distributors are not the end of the story.

What about the companies that package and manufacture (can, box, bottle, and bag) food for sale to restaurants?

They have life and death economic decisions to make too.

If their customers, the food distributors, are not ordering at normal levels, does it make sense for them to keep a full staff on the payroll and factories at full operation? Can they even afford to if they want to?

The problem they face is obvious. Can they afford to assume the considerable costs necessary to produce a product for customers who may not be in a position to order anything next week, next month, next season?

The ripple effect goes back further.

Farmers.

For many farmers, especially, but not limited to, small independent farmers, the restaurant industry is their prized cash cow. Restaurants provide big orders, steady demand, and streamline their distribution costs.

What do they do if food manufacturers and restaurants aren't buying?

We've already seen news stories of farmers pouring tankers of milk into sewers and plowing under thousands of acres of perfectly good crops.

They're not doing this to be mean. They're doing it because it costs real money to harvest and transport food – and they've lost a big piece of the market they planned to sell it to.

Now, right now this month, farmers have to make the decision: Do they "roll the dice" and spend the money necessary to put in crops this spring for a demand that may not exist come this summer and fall?

Farmers in turn are served by truckers who in turn provide work for tens of thousands driving and maintaining fleets.

And fertilizer companies and farm equipment sellers. Their sales are down. With sales and service down, do they need all the employees they're carrying?

Then there is this fact of life:

All these people – the restaurant owners, restaurant employees, food suppliers and their employees, food manufacturers and their employees, farmers and their employees, agricultural service companies and their employees – have debt. Debt that they expected to be able to service and pay off with normal earnings.

Clearly that's out the window – and not just for the 20 million people who have lost their jobs, but also for the businesses that are still marginally "open."

What happens when the banks who have lent to those tens of millions of people and entities stop receiving payments? Those payments are necessary for new credit to be issued. Once loans start defaulting the overall availability of credit diminishes and becomes more expensive.

And that's just the ripples from the restaurant industry.

We haven't talked about what it means when retail stores are shut down. That's another 10% of the workforce and like the impact of restaurant closures, it kicks off its own chain reaction: wholesales, truckers, manufacturers, designers, cotton farmers.

And this is the scenario for the "lucky" countries.

As traumatic as forced unemployment is in the developed world, it is an immediate life-threatening catastrophe in the developing world.

Why?

In the words of a Guatemalan who explained it to me years ago:

"In the US, I work for a day and I can afford groceries for a whole week. In Guatemala, the same work only earns me food for that day – and not much else."

One day of no work means immediate hunger in the developing world. That day started several weeks ago.

I'm not presenting this as an exercise in "the sky is falling."

It's a cold, hard look at the reality of "The Shutdown." A reality we are not getting from the news and even some otherwise astute financial people.

We have faced serious pandemics before, a simple fact the news media is obscuring, but no one has ever suggested - let alone ordered - a prolonged indefinite shutdown of the global economy as a response.

Did you know that in 1957-58, there was a thing called "The Asian Flu?" It killed a million or more globally. It was a pandemic too and killed tens of thousands of Americans.

Did you know that in 1968-70, there was a thing called "The Hong Kong Flu?" It killed a million or more globally as well. Another pandemic that killed tens of thousands of Americans.

Nothing was shut down for that, including the Vietnam War.

During the Hong Kong Flu Pandemic, the US had over 500,000 soldiers in Asia, some living under the difficult and less-than-sanitary conditions of combat deployment.

The US government at that time saw no need to panic and applied common sense precautions: hand washing, advising the sick to stay home and rest, treating the serious cases, etc.

Yes, there is a pandemic.

Yes, the public needs to apply caution and common sense – something in my experience they are doing very well, despite the news media's endless hunt for exceptions.

Yes, this pandemic is going to kill some vulnerable people, in this case overwhelmingly people with pre-existing health conditions.

Yes, the medical system will be strained in some places during particular periods.

These things happen periodically. They are inconvenient, disruptive and for the people and their families directly affected, tragic.

I'm not going to say these things are "normal", but they clearly fall within the spectrum of known human experience.

What is not normal – and I am hard pressed to think of or find another single example in all of human history – is forcibly shutting down at least 50% (but probably much more) of the life-sustaining business activities of humanity for a prolonged and indefinite period of time, and thinking "the government" can somehow magically solve it by printing money to plug the gaps.

As I said on this month's extended System Club call, we're trying to fill Lake Superior with a fire hose. The amounts being spent may look like a lot – and they are – but they are inadequate for the task.

The idea that government financial manipulation can somehow underwrite the economic health of a shuttered US economy for weeks, let alone months, is a dangerous delusion.

The people smoking this delusion-provoking "crack" are, not so coincidentally, people who draw steady paychecks from the government or the media outlet they read the news for and have no idea how the real world actually works.

For now, at least, these people are in control of the country.

We start taking the country back by taking back our language.

The gravest danger facing us now is not "The Pandemic" real as it may be. It's "The Shutdown." The unplanned for, poorly conceived, irrational and indefinite "Shutdown."

Let's start calling the period we're living through right now what it really is.

Call it "The Shutdown" not "The Pandemic," focus on the big picture, and let's start getting ourselves and our communities ready to go back to the work of serving people with the things they need.

We're going to rebuild this country, not the government. Yes, the news media and people angling for political advantage will tell us we're wrong every step of the way.

Screw 'em and do the right thing.

A thought experiment

April 26, 2020

The doorbell rings.

You look out and lo and behold, it's "America's favorite doctor" Tony Fauci with an assistant holding a clipboard.

Of course, you open the door and let him in.

"Hello Dr. Fauci. What can I do for you?" you ask.

"As you know there is a deadly pandemic sweeping the world," he starts in his calm, rational, well modulated tones.

"Yes, I know. People with immunosuppressive diseases, advanced diabetes, morbid obesity and other medical disorders are at risk – just as they are of every disease including the common cold."

For a split second, he frowns, but regains his composure quickly.

"Based on genetic testing, we've determined that even though you're pretty healthy, you've got a rare genetic predisposition that makes you as vulnerable as a nursing home patient in a wheelchair with dementia and advanced stage four cancer."

Understandably, the news hits you hard and you feel your knees start to buckle. You take hold of the wall to brace yourself. Then you take a deep breath, clear your mind, and ask a logical question.

"Is there anything I can do to protect myself?"

"I'm glad you asked. Yes. To reduce the odds that your life might be shortened, we recommend the following: shut down at least 50% of the world economy and have everyone shelter in place until we know we're all safe."

You, of course, want to live, but you want to make sure you heard what Dr. Fauci said correctly.

"Won't that plunge a billion or more people into poverty worldwide? Won't that financially destroy hundreds of thousands of small business owners and their families in America alone? Won't that put a $50 trillion hole in the world economy?"

(You know a little about poverty, having been on the "meal-every-other-day" plan for several months when one of your businesses failed when you were a young man.

You've also traveled the world, gone way off the beaten track and seen first hand that the real poverty millions live in is more horrifying than anything that ever makes it to the TV set.)

"You can't put a value on a single human life," Dr. Fauci says, so confident, so sure, so calm, so reasonable.

"And what about that 'indefinite' part? When does this thing you're proposing end?" you ask.

"When everyone is 100% completely safe, we'll let you know. It could be weeks, it could be months, it could be years. We don't know right now."

Now, the person with a clipboard has a question for you.

"We can only go ahead with your approval. Please sign here where it's marked 'x' and date it and we'll start the shutdown right away."

The ball's in your court now.

In order to prevent something that may or may not happen to you and squeeze out a few more years, maybe even a few more decades, all you have to do is agree to rain incalculable misery down on hundreds of millions of people for an indefinite period of time...

What do you do?

Of course, we all have a strong self-preservation instinct. It's one of the most important things we've got.

But, before you make up your mind, you sit down and think things through.

You've got a big decision to make.

You can be the cause of hundreds of millions of people not getting the medical care they need and dying or becoming disabled prematurely. You can be the cause of hundreds of millions of kids spending their formative years malnourished and as a result suffer permanent brain and health disorders the rest of their lives. You can be the cause of hundreds of millions being denied the chance for a life with a modicum of dignity.

Or, you can take your chances, take self-protective measures, and keep the world economy going and doing its admittedly less-than-perfect-but-not-terribly-bad job of feeding, housing, educating and providing health care for billions of people.

I'm sure there are some monsters out there who think that their convenience and grinding out a few extra years is worth this price, but thankfully, there aren't many.

But the proposition was never put to you this way, was it?

Instead it was put in terms of "grandma."

"You don't want to kill your grandma, do you?"

First, did anyone ask grandma if improving her chances of living a few more years – assuming she is vulnerable to CoVid-2 at all – is worth devastating the lives of hundreds of millions of people?

Most grandmas I've known, including my own, may they rest in peace, would answer that question even more emphatically than a healthy young person.

"My grandchildren living in an impoverished world, deprived of good work, or education, or access to health care, so I can get a few extra years? HELL NO!"

But no one in the "news" media asked a grandma that question, did they?

We were just told to "think about grandma" and "how could you do something that might kill her?"

This demonic piece of mental sleight of hand is the justification behind the biggest financial catastrophe of the last 100 years – maybe the last 250 years – maybe ever.

It will result in illness, premature death, and amputated opportunities for millions of people worldwide, with an especially brutal impact on the young.

And none of it is medically or scientifically justified. This isn't pleasant stuff to contemplate.

It would sure be nice not to have to exert ourselves wrapping our minds around all this stuff, but if we don't think our collective backs are to the wall and we all need to do some serious thinking, we're not paying attention.

We – not the news media, not universities, not the government, not even industry experts – figured out how to make the Internet a viable medium that increased opportunities for education and business exponentially for billions over what existed before it.

We're certainly all capable of blowing through the current news media-generated hysteria and working through the issues ourselves, especially when the stakes are as high as they are.

An imaginary conversation
May 01, 2020

"We are all going to DIE!!!"

How do you even begin to communicate with people like this?

Here's an idea.

"Tell me. What's your degree in?"

"Communications and a minor in political science."

"Great! But you took some science and math courses, right?"

"Well, uh, I took a Geology class."

"Great! But you've continued your self-education since, right?"

"Of course."

"What's the last book you've read about immunology or epidemiology?"

"What? Who reads about stuff like that?"

"OK. How about general books on science?"

"Who has time for that? It's not my thing."

"OK. So you're going along with the shutdown of the economy, the bankrupting of millions of people and businesses, the devastation of hundreds of millions of people in the developing world based on what exactly?"

"What are you an idiot? Everyone knows. It's the virus! The Virus!! The VIRUS!!! We're all going to die!!!"

"You've talked to doctors of course."

"Of course!"

"Actually talked with them?"

"Well, I've seen them on TV."

"That's great!

So you followed up on everything they said to confirm it's true? And then looked into their backgrounds to see why they might be taking one position or another?

And sought out and heard opinions from other equally – or even more – credible people?"

"Of course not. What do you think I am? Some kind of nut?"

"Well, I'm glad you asked the question, not me."

There are news stories that don't involve you and generally it makes sense to avoid them.

That said, Tony Fauci's Great CoVid-19 Pandemic (Episode 11 of his "The Viruses are Coming to Get Us" Series) is one of those stories you need to pay attention to.

I could be wrong, but from where I sit every responsible adult has a duty to look at this one.

And when you do, you're going to discover a super abundance of problems with the official story.

I'm sure anyone who has ever had the dubious pleasure of doing business with the news media knows they get things wrong.

Guess what?

They do it with everything - and the more money on the table, the more wrong they get it. (They're funny that way.)

And if, for whatever reason, they don't want to hear something, they just ignore it.

And if that doesn't work, they censor it.

A fews days ago, I posted a press conference by a veteran California physician who operates a network that treats tens of thousands of patients a year.

Apparently someone at Google/YouTube didn't like it so it was removed.

Thanks to the magic of the Internet…it's back.

Here's the kind of thing "they don't want you to know" literally. (Not a clever headline. Really. They don't want you to know.)

Facts for the fearful

[Links to these videos available on page: https://KenMcCarthy.com/blog/an-imaginary-conversation]

- **The death projections were crazy – and we know that now**

- **Lockdown vs No lockdown, No difference**

- **The cost of social isolation**

- **The Pandemic vs the Annual Flu**

- **How the lock down damages the immune system**

- **Sheltering in place, masks, and gloves are not helping you**

- **Deliberately distorted death statistics**

- **The extreme medical illogic of quarantining the healthy**

- **No reason to continue the shutdown**

These are not the only doctors, epidemiologists, and immunologists saying these things.

If I had an extra 20 hours a week, I could load this page with many, many more.

I found these guys especially interesting because they work with patients, are directors of a large chain of urgent care clinics, and Google/YouTube found that their comments "violated community standards."

That's the world we're in right now.

I'm spending time on this topic because it doesn't appear the world is going to get back to work until the virus – of ignorance, official lying, panic, and hysteria – is cured.

I'm doing my bit.

I hope these articles help you do yours.

Profiles in courage: Dr. Dan Erickson and Dr. Artin Massihi

May 04, 2020

The "response" to the pandemic has been politicized, commercialized and propped up with garbage science since day one. The fact that it is still dragging on with no end in sight – over four weeks after what we were told was a two week "pause to flatten the curve" – is predictable based on this fact.

The heroes of this story are the independent doctors, nurses and public representatives who are speaking out.

They are few and far between and they are paying an enormous personal price.

Note: These are doctors in private practice and owners of their own clinics.

Small business people.

Us.

The people who are holding things together in the face of an onslaught of self-serving news media and political people - the Dirty Duo of society.

One of the many odd things about all this is that in normal times, the average person holds both TV news readers

45

and politicians in very low regard. They are among the least trusted members of society, and rightly so.

Their temporary ascendence is a tribute to the power of pushing the "fear" button, something they're doing daily with one set of misrepresentations and fabrications after another.

Every day, they float a new story of doom. Some stick. Some go down in flames without impact.

If you actually track them, they're virtually all based on exaggeration, misrepresentation of data, and blanket censorship of any analysis that doesn't agree with their narrative – even when that analysis comes from Nobel Prize winners and other eminent scientists.

Commentary from original post

I've received concerned emails from physicians that the doctors who talked about Immunology 101 in a press conference on a page I posted Sunday have been "viciously condemned" and "sanctioned" by medical authorities.

First, the "sanction" is one page (two paragraphs) posted anonymously to a medical association website.

Second, it comes from the equivalent of a trade association, not a medical society.

Third, if there were a sanctions "case" against these two doctors, it sure was fast. If it's tried and settled, what was the charge and where's the evidence that anything they said was inaccurate?

This is the unsigned claim against them:

"These reckless and untested musings do not speak for medical society and are inconsistent with current science and epidemiology regarding COVID-19."

"Reckless and untested" reading of publicly available statistics?

"Reckless and untested" recitation of the principles of Immunology 101?

"Inconsistent with current science and epidemiology regarding COVID-19."

Science? What "science" has been applied to COVID-19 reporting? I'll grant that there's been a lot of amateur hysteria.

As for epidemiology, the trade association could not find a single epidemiologist to put his or her name to this thing. Cowardice personified.

But there's more from these clowns:

"As owners of local urgent care clinics, it appears these two individuals are releasing biased, non-peer reviewed data to advance their personal financial interests without regard for the public's health."

It "appears"?

They either did something wrong or they didn't. Don't tell me what "appears."

If the "crime" is not defined, then the "conviction" is worse than a bad joke.

Additionally, can somebody show me the unbiased, peer reviewed data that justifies shutting the world economy down and quarantining healthy people over a seasonal respiratory illness that has a death rate in the ballpark of annual influenza?

No such peer reviewed data exists.

If this all weren't so tragic, I'd laugh.

To get email from doctors backing this sad PR bullshit up and advising me to remove my article is pathetic and preposterous.

For anyone who calls himself a doctor not to take the time to advise him or herself about what is going on in regards to this particular claim of "killer pandemic" in a serious way is despicable.

You expect that from the news media. You expect that from politicians. You expect that from the terrorized man in the street.

But from doctors?

Bottom line: Some doctors have brains and spines and aren't content to play the "go along to get along" game. They're the only heroes in this story.

As for others, well, don't ever assume the advice you get from a doctor is anything better than you'd get from a random drunk on a park bench.

Second, third and fourth opinion everything a doctor tells you when the treatment involves drugs or surgery. Find out what the downside is. Find out what the alternatives are.

You better know what they're doing, because nine times out of ten *they* don't. Most of the time. Their mercantile incompetence is just an annoyance. Other times, it could kill or cripple you.

Every year there are 100,000 or more reported deaths from infections caught IN US HOSPITALS. Every year. And that's just the tip if the iceberg of systemic medical incompetence.

American doctors have a lot to answer for.

Our costs are at least twice as high as anywhere else in the world and **we don't even rate as a developed nation in global health stats.**

I think every doctor in this system should take at least one day in their careers where they do something other than selling out their patients in the interest of preserving consensus mediocrity and their own skins.

We are making decisions that will destroy millions of people's economic foundation for many, many years to come. This will come with a heavy price in health, mental, and physical suffering.

We're telling perfectly healthy people to behave as if they are late stage AIDS patients with no immune systems: 1) stay locked away in their homes, 2) avoid interaction with other healthy people, 3) wear surgical masks everywhere they go even when walking down the street alone, and 4) stay out of parks and off the beach.

Worst of all, people are being advised to get their health information about what's going on from television and from a guy named Tony Fauci who has a long history of exaggerating public health scares for personal aggrandizement. (See AIDS, H1NI, Ebola, Zika.)

More about him later.

Almost the last word – Taking a close look at Tony Fauci & Co.

May 05, 2020

In case you haven't noticed, Anthony "Tony" Fauci is leading the Pandemic Parade.

He's the source of the "reason" for shutting down the world economy – including preventive and necessary medical services – for nearly the last two months.

He has, in a very real sense, become the unelected dictator of the world.

Do you think I'm exaggerating?

He determines what is acceptable behavior and what is not.

Going to War-Mart – acceptable. Going to Church – unacceptable. He decides who you can do business with (Amazon) and who you cannot (local retail stores.)

If that isn't dictatorial powers, I don't know what is.

You'd have to reach back to people like Stalin or Mao to find someone who exerted anything close to this level of control over daily life.

Believe it or not, despite the news media's heroic attempts to not educate you – or even raise the issue – Tony Fauci has a history.

A long history.

He is not liked or admired – and certainly not trusted – by many of the great scientists of our time.

Here's one example:

Nobel Prize winner Kary Mullis is the inventor of the polymerase chain reaction technique or PCR.

This is the very technique that Fauci and others used to "prove" that a single virus (HIV) causes the over thirty different diseases called "AIDS".

Ten full years after Fauci & Co's 1984 announcement that they had "discovered the virus that causes AIDS," Mullis called their science "make believe" and nothing more than a politicized, money making scam.

Unfortunately, thanks to very aggressive PR, which included destroying the careers of scientists with differing views, the public was carefully fooled into going along with the scammers and not the science.

Thirty six years and hundreds of billions of dollars later, the "science" Fauci claimed he had has still not produced the AIDS vaccine he told us was "right around the corner" in 1984.

Whipping up the idiot news media into a frenzy is what Anthony Fauci does.

He's a multi-decade master of it.

However, this time, instead of burning down a house or a block, in this his latest stunt, he's burned down the whole city.

Actually, it's worse.

There's not a city or town in this world that isn't going to be left holding a multi-million or multi-billion dollar bag of financial damages when this is over.

The last time he pulled this, it resulted in lawsuits against pharmaceutical companies for unduly panicking European countries into buying tens of millions of doses of vaccine which turned out to be completely unnecessary.

Additional References

Early March: What Fauci said to Congress:
https://justthenews.com/politics-policy/coronavirus/fauci-offers-more-conservative-death-rate-academic-article-public-virus

Late March: What Fauci said to the New England Journal of Medicine
https://www.nejm.org/doi/full/10.1056/NEJMe2002387

The CDC's actual death count minus the PR department hysteria
https://www.cdc.gov/nchs/nvss/vsrr/covid19/index.htm

Instructions to doctors (the CDC's own document): "Just call it COVID019 and call it a day."
https://www.cdc.gov/nchs/data/nvss/coronavirus/Alert-2-New-ICD-code-introduced-for-COVID-19-deaths.pdf

US MDs report on what actually works...ignored by CDC which continues to recommend methods that some believe are injuring and killing patients: "Avoid intubation if possible"
https://www.evms.edu/media/evms_public/departments/internal_medicine/EVMS_Critical_Care_COVID-19_Protocol.pdf

Virus Mania: How the Medical Industry Continually Invents Epidemics, Making Billion-Dollar Profits At Our Expense

Experts who are being ignored

The news media has not and will put these people on television, but they will give every "fright night" hack a national platform to fill the public with dread and confusion.

David Katz – Yale University Professor Preventive Medicine and Public Health. Author of textbook on epidemiology

John Ioannidis – Stanford University C.F. Rehnborg Chair in Disease Prevention, Professor of Medicine, of

Epidemiology and Population Health, and (by courtesy) of Biomedical Data Science, and of Statistics; co-Director, Meta-Research Innovation Center at Stanford (METRICS).

Johan Giesecke – Advisor to the government of Sweden Swedish physician and Professor Emeritus at the Karolinska Institute in Stockholm. Member of the Strategic and Technical Advisory Group for Infectious Hazards (WHO)

Knut Wittoski – Head of Rockefeller Universities of Biostatistics, Epidemiology and Research Design for twenty years (emeritus)

Michael Levitt – Professor of Structural Biology at the Stanford School of Medicine, Winner of the 2013 Nobel Prize for Chemistry for "the development of multiscale models for complex chemical systems."

Why have I spent so much time on this issue?

Because it's a multi-trillion dollar issue.

Frankly, I can't understand why any person with the time, resources and ability would not take up this study.

We are where we are largely because too many people have kept their heads down and "minded their own business."

We've abdicated responsibility for the most fundamental issues in our lives.

We've given up responsibility for our health to a corrupt and incompetent medial industry.

We've allowed our financial system to be run for the benefit of a few Wall Street banks and to the detriment of every other segment of the economy.

And worst of all, we've let television and its evil twin, so called "social media", do our thinking and research for us.

We sowed the wind with this neglect and now we're reaping the whirlwind.

It's past time to man (or woman) up, don't you think?

Signs of sanity returning

May 27, 2020

Lawsuits, articulate letters from Senators to the President, growing protests – and most important all – growing awareness.

Back in late March, I gave advice for how to deal with what we were told was going to be a two week shutdown.

Since then, I've continuously pointed out that any continuation beyond the initial "curve flattening" is based on inexcusable fraud.

I've "lost" quite a few subscribers over my statements and I have two things to say about that:

1. Don't let the door hit your ass on the way out.

2. If you agree with the "public health" measures of Tony Fauci, a serially inept and corrupt Washington DC bureaucrat/politician, please unsubscribe. I don't want to assist you in making money nor even more importantly, survive long enough to reproduce more like you.

I've never thought of ignorance as a crime, but I've changed my mind on this.

To maintain ignorance as to the basic shape of this fraud and support even one more second of this mad economic shutdown is criminal conduct of the most reckless and vicious kind.

For the rest of us, the human beings who don't have our heads so far up our ass we can't see daylight, we have a lot of work to do:

...Not only to recover our own businesses, but to generate the resources we need to give aid – ongoing aid – to our neighbors, our communities, our fellow small business people, and to the most vulnerable.

We have to be smarter and stronger and work and contribute like we have never worked and contributed before.

If you're looking for a place to start helping, get acquainted with your local food bank.

This is going to be a multi-year reconstruction process.

Current stock market bullshit aside (because it is total bullshit), the basic fabric of our economy – putting bread on the table – has been savagely torn for many, many millions of people and it is not going to be easy or fast to mend.

YOU, the small business owner, the backbone of society, have never been more important.

With that in mind, I'll keep you posted with ongoing interviews with remarkable entrepreneurs, advisors and educators. I've got a great one coming up soon. Stay tuned.

Meanwhile, if you want to educate yourself, so that you are never, ever again scammed by Tony Fauci and his ilk, I've put a video together that covers just a tiny fraction of one of the frauds he and his gang have been involved in in the past and their catastrophic human cost.

This material is heavy lifting, but ignorance on these matters has proven to be catastrophically expensive. We must never allow this kind of thing to happen again, not to us, not to any group of people.

If you find this material useful, please send me positive feedback. Putting these things together is very time and labor intensive and like everyone else, I can use some encouragement from time to time.

Who the hell is Tony Fauci and why did we annihilate the world economy based on his say so?

June 05, 2020

Things are fast-breaking in the Coronavirus Con.

Unfortunately, the important news is being drowned out by ecstatic announcements about "progress" in the vaccine gold rush.

What are you not being told?

Just this…

The central data source that was used to judge CoVid-19 drug trials was fabricated by an MD and Internet con artist named Sapan Desai.

As a result, The Lancet, one of the world's most important medical journals, has removed one published study and is looking at more that used his data as their source.

Does this matter?

It sure does.

Using this data, low cost – and unpatentable – drugs with decades of clinical use by hundreds of millions were rejected, while expensive, experimental, proprietary drugs in classes that are known to have dangerous toxicity were promoted.

Not my theory, a report from a UK newspaper The Guardian.

(Link to article here: https://www.theguardian.com/world/2020/jun/03/covid-19-surgisphere-wworld-health-organization-hydroxychloroquine)

But this story is being ignored which is why I'm sharing it with you.

Does it matter?

I don't know. You tell me.

Does being aware of the fundamental facts that underlie your reality matter?

Originally written June 1, 2020

Tony Robbins released a video last week with some of the experts we highlighted over a month ago who suggested that not only has the shutdown gone on too long (no kidding!), but there was no good reason for a shutdown in the first place.

Actually, the problem goes much deeper than that.

System Club members have been aware of the central issues for quite some time.

Now, at last I have enough of a critical mass of documentation to make a public statement that the CoVid Con was not an honest mistake, but rather part of a pattern of fraud that mirrors other frauds that Tony Fauci and his network have been engaging in for over 36 years.

Like all complicated scams, it takes some time and effort to unpack, but as you'll see, I am not making an idle or unsubstantiated claim.

It's unnerving to realize that one band of criminals – the pharmaceutical industry – could have this kind of power over our lives, but as you'll see, they do.

Why other major industries – banking, energy, manufacturing, travel and retail etc. – have tolerated this disruption of their operations and the destruction of trillions of dollars of their equity is beyond me.

WHO comes clean: "Asymptomatic carriers don't spread CoVid"

June 08, 2020

It's official.

Tony Fauci responds

June 09, 2020

Last night I related the report from the World Health Organization that finally admitted that the SCIENCE shows that spread of CoVid by asymptomatic "carriers" is very rare.

To a thinking person, this calls into question: why then we shut down – and continue to shut down – the world economy at the cost of incalculable human suffering globally if only symptomatic people spread the disease?

This is Fauci's answer to that $15 to $50 trillion dollar question:

"Yeah, I think a lot of confusion has emanated from this issue of an asymptomatic person and asymptomatic transmission. When you look at the number of people - if you look at all the cases of coronavirus infection, about 25 to even up to 45% of the people are asymptomatic. The real question is, what is the percentage of infections that go from an asymptomatic person to an uninfected person. And that's something that we know that occurs, but we're really not sure exactly what the extent of it is. Because it's very difficult to measure that. You can determine how many asymptomatic people there are merely by doing screenings and finding out - but when you're doing epidemiology... So what the WHO said yesterday, that, although there are asymptomatic infections, and although asymptomatic people can transmit, they are not the drivers of the outbreak. The drivers of the outbreak are people who are symptomatic, and transmit to others. That doesn't mean that asymptomatic transmission doesn't play a role. But it isn't the major driver of the outbreak. And yet there's this confusion when people talk about who's asymptomatic infection and who's driving it. But that's really what the WHO meant."

Note that Yahoo had a financial reporter interview Fauci, not a medical or science reporter. Speaks volumes, doesn't it?

What I'm doing with the federal blood money

June 12, 2020

After some thought, I decided against setting fire to the federal government's CoVid blood money check and instead used it to buy an ad in a locally owned magazine that focuses on local issues.

Here's the ad:

Better times are coming – if we make them

Things you can do to help…

1. For fifty years, Family of Woodstock has been housing, feeding, and serving our brothers and sisters in need in Ulster County. The need for their services has exploded exponentially: Familyofwoodstockinc.org

2. If you're lucky enough to be on dry land financially, spend locally and lavishly like you've never done before.

3. The June issue of the Chronogram offered some of the best coverage of "The Pandemic" in any format and from any source. You can subscribe to them for home delivery. A

$36-a-year vote of confidence for people who are watching your back.

4. Buy and read the book "Virus Mania" (2007) by Claus Kohnlein MD and Torsten Engelbrecht. We can no longer afford to leave issues of health up to mass media reporting and other unreliable sources.

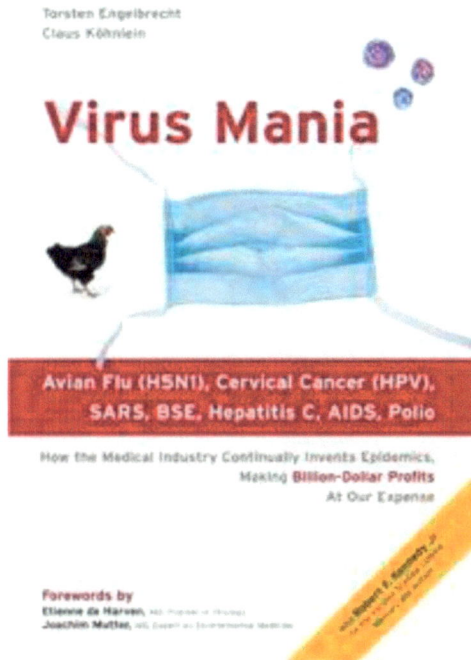

Black lives matter to politicians... unless they're small business owners

June 16, 2020

How many thousands of small businesses are literally being choked to death, not by a virus, or by a thug wearing a police uniform, but by despotic politicians who are using CoVid to throw their weight around?

The reality is that the food and restaurant business has long been a chance for creative, hard working people of all backgrounds to create livelihoods for themselves and their communities.

These important, hard working people who do so much to make our lives more pleasant are being economically murdered in broad daylight.

In New York City, and no doubt in other places where tyrants rule, restaurants are not allowed to use sidewalks – the sidewalks their exorbitant tax bills pay for – without massive red tape and permissions, all of which are currently shut down.

Rather than show basic common sense and decency, politicians and bureaucrats are maintaining their petty chokeholds.

Chapter 2

Lockdowns "To Flatten The Curve"

Unraveling The CoVid Con

The mask thing is a sinister fraud

July 06, 2020

There are some – not many – but some people with intelligence, integrity and courage.

One US public official out of millions – Democratic mayor of Nevada City, California Reinette Senum – is willing to fall on her sword to tell the public the truth.

When Fauci and the U.S. Surgeon General told the truth

Medical science and practice has not changed since they originally said these things.

The CDC's own report

"In pooled analysis, we found no significant reduction in influenza transmission with the use of face masks"

https://wwwnc.cdc.gov/eid/article/26/5/19-0994_article?fbclid=IwAR2V1hPqN0WKb2kXVExP_1UE9A Rvru6mtPZvZN0w1jx0S3l3fXLhxMP_bXs

Profiles in Courage – Scott Jensen MD

July 06, 2020

In my last post (July 6, 2020), I featured the Democratic mayor of Nevada City, California Reinette Senum who put herself, her career, and her standing on the line in her hometown, to tell her neighbors and fellow citizens what public health officials told her about masks: 1) they don't work and 2) there are serious health consequences if used incorrectly.

It occurs to me in this era of blatant medical fraud and widespread cowardice, one thing I can do is feature the informed people who are not going along with this, not waiting for "officials" to come to their senses, and not pretending what is in practice a global crime against humanity is not taking place.

Today's profile in courage Dr. Scott Jensen MD.

Dr. Scott Jensen is a practicing MD with thirty-five years of practice. He's also a State Senator from Minnesota.

He is the whistleblower who called fraud on the instructions Minnesota doctors were given ordering them to falsify cause of death records in such a way as to boost deaths "from CoVid."

As a result of Dr. Jensen's courage, Minnesota was shamed into recording the cause of deaths during the pandemic accurately.

Profiles in courage – Richard Bartlett, MD

July 12, 2020

Does the medical industrial complex suppress simple, safe, inexpensive, and effective treatments in favor of expensive, patented, dangerous ones that cause more problems than they solve?

Yes they do.

It's called the "standard of care" and it's something I've been talking with System Club members about for years, long before the CoVid Con.

It's great for the pharmaceutical and medical devices industry. Not so great for us.

Through the magic of a process called "agency capture," pharmaceutical and medical devices dictate to physicians how they may and how they may not treat diseases.

Would you believe the "standard of care" always errs on the side of things that make a boatload of money for the Medical Industrial Complex? Funny how that works.

There are many books about this and you can confirm this with your own research. One place to start might be "Is

74

Your Cardiologist Killing You?" by Sherry Rogers MD, a physician with over 50 years of clinical experience.

Why do I routinely cover material like this in the System Club?

Because success is a triad: 1) money making, 2) wealth preservation and building, and 3) health. Part One is just the front end of the system.

As System Club members know, behind the closed doors of the Club, I hammer on items #2 and #3 routinely.

I've easily spent at least as much time studying them, probably much more, than I've ever spent studying marketing – and I've spent a lot of time studying marketing.

Why?

Because within the bounds of mortality, I expect to win and my job is to help my clients to win, too.

It's hard to win if you're sick or prematurely dead.

Life's hard enough without handing the bad guys a gun to shoot you with – and that pretty much sums up what happens to people who hand over their fate to our medical and financial systems.

Just as it is in the operation of your business, ignorance about finances and health is a very expensive self indulgence.

Profiles in Courage – Erin Marie Olszewski, RN

July 18, 2020

New York City had exponentially more deaths per capita from CoVid than any other place on earth. Way beyond anything that makes sense statistically.

Why did so many New Yorker City residents die?

Astonishingly, no one in the news media is asking this question.

But there is an answer.

Some brave nurses, doctors and techs have come forward to explain.

My conversation with a true hero Erin Marie Olszewski, RN.

https://www.youtube.com/watch?v=bcxD8byr5is

Note: I have seen the inside of a city-run public hospital and once had to go to an emergency room as a patient in a New York City hospital. What Erin and other out-of-town contract nurses, techs, and doctors have said about what they saw rings true with my experience.

Three voices

July 23, 2020

At this late date, the only way anyone can possibly continue to support what is going on right now is if they are ignorant about fundamentals of law, medicine, and/or history.

Nothing that is being done related to CoVid conforms to any previously acceptable medical practice. It's all in blatant violation of the most basic civil rights law as well.

But somehow it's all OK "because there's a virus."

This is dangerous idiocy of the highest order.

Three speakers: an active emergency room physician who happens to be a lawyer too, a doctor who runs a large clinic in Ohio, and a sensible person who has a grasp of the flow of history.

Simone Gold MD, JD

Pam Popper PhD, ND

Polly St. George

Digging deep into the CoVid Con

August 09, 2020

I get that some people are trying to "do the right thing."

But at some point, when do you wake up and admit you're enabling a colossal fraud and literal crime against humanity?

It's August.

The "crisis," which started in March, was supposed to last two weeks to "flatten the curve."

What do we have to show for our efforts?

Continued and even escalating hysteria fueled by an irresponsible news media, encouraged by politicians, and enabled by people who should know better.

Here's a multi-trillion dollar question that clarifies things.

How did Sweden do?

It's almost impossible to get clear information from the US news media, but if you dig you can find it.

Sweden temporarily banned gatherings of more than 50, they encouraged – but did not command – work from home, and they moved high school and college classes online.

Here's what they did not do.

They did not shut down day care and primary schools. They did not order businesses closed, though they did ask restaurants to provide more space between tables. No one was told to "lock down" or stay home. No one was compelled to wear masks.

The outcome?

Sweden won.

Their death rate is lower than countries like Spain, France, the UK and the US which took idiotic and ruinous measures and continue this day to extend them.

As important, Sweden has achieved herd immunity, the ever-reliable force of nature that solves problems like this every single time they occur and always has since before recorded history.

What about the countries that went into "lockdown" mode, put everyone in masks, and ruined their economies?

Not only did these countries fail to "stop the spread," they're now having "second waves" as they try and fail to re-open from their excessive and misguided shutdowns.

Sweden is having no such problem.

This outcome was predictable and indeed was predicated back in April.

In case you miss it, here's the question this Swedish scientist asked smug Australian newscasters back in April:

"How are you and 100 other countries going to come OUT of your lockdowns without having achieved herd immunity?"

The CoVid Con is the product of a medical/scientific fraud machine that's been operating in high gear for 36 years though its roots are much older. Fauci is the tip of the iceberg of thousands of "professionals" who make their livings misleading the public & pumping hysteria.

Until the public gets a handle on this reality, there is no way out of this thing. It can't be explained in a 10 second sound bite, but for people who care (does that include any so-called journalists?), it's all neatly tied up in the video below.

A DEEP dive into the sinister career of serial medical con artist Tony Fauci who is culpable in the death of hundreds of thousands, perhaps millions, of people.

Think I'm exaggerating?

Watch this 90 minute film and learn what informed people have known about this guy for decades which somehow only the news media and politicians – and the people foolish enough to believe them – don't know.

Here's the narrative:

A deadly new virus is discovered...there's no treatment or cure...it's highly contagious...everyone is a potential victim...the world is at risk from asymptomatic super spreaders...new clusters of cases reported daily...

Everyone must get tested even though the tests are unreliable...positive antibody tests are called "infections" and "cases" even when the patient has no symptoms...every politician gets involved...media hysteria in high gear...activists demand salvation from the government and Big Pharma...

Billions of dollars are authorized for fast track drug and vaccine research...simple, effective remedies are rejected while expensive, dangerous ones are pushed......presumptive diagnoses...exaggerated death statistics...falsified death certificates...

Covid 2020?

No. HIV=AIDS in the 1980s.

Every single fraud technique being used today to "sell" CoVid hysteria was invented in the 1980s and 1990s by Tony Fauci and Friends to sell the HIV=AIDS fraud.

Are you surprised to hear HIV=AIDS called a fraud? You won't be after you watch this film. As an added bonus, all this CoVid madness will suddenly make a lot more sense: Fauci's First Fraud

https://www.youtube.com/watch?v=wy3frBacd2k

99% of the population has made the fundamental mistake of watching the puppets and not paying attention to the strings.

Time to look at the strings.

Game over

August 30, 2020

It's late August.

We're five plus months into an enforced shutdown of economic, social, religious and even medical activity that has rained suffering (in some cases premature death) down on countless hundreds of millions, even billions, of people.

Suicides are up, bankruptcies are up, business failures are up, unemployment is up, hunger is up – and there's no end in sight.

And finally, after all this time, the front man, the chief con artist, admits to the public something every reasonably informed person knew in March: Asymptomatic people do not spread disease.

In other words, if you do not have the symptoms of a disease – fever, fatigue, coughing and sneezing – you're not going to spread a disease.

So why was society shut down?

Why are people being told to wear masks 24/7 and avoid normal contact with each other?

Why are schools, businesses, and churches still shut down?

Why are people with no symptoms being told they need to be tested and why does a positive antibody test in symptomless people (i.e. asymptomatic) trigger hysteria and justification for prolonging the shutdown?

There's no medical sense here – and there never was.

Top epidemiologists from places like Stanford, Yale, and leading Europe universities were on record when this thing started that a shutdown was misguided and would do significant harm. The news media ignored them.

Statistics clearly show the nature of this pandemic. It is, in fact, a bad flu.

Here are typical stats from Princeton, a town in one of the "hot spot" states, New Jersey.

28,000 population. 18 CoVid "related" deaths, which is different from deaths from CoVid but we'll use the number anyway. This makes a per capita death rate 0.06%. The average age of death is 84.6 – in a state where the life expectancy is 80 years.

How is this by any standard other than fraud-driven hysteria a public health emergency that merits the extreme measures being taken?

How can such a thing be taking place?

Five reasons:

1. The abysmal level of ignorance among the average person about very basic issues of health and hygiene.

84

It would be hard to imagine a level of ignorance more profound.

2. The existence of a large network of people – bureaucrats, pharmaceutical industry executives, PR and ad agency executives, so-called "news" agencies, academics, "scientists", and politicians of all stripes – who, in exchange for a paycheck and career security, are willing to sell out humanity on behalf of the interests of the Medical Industrial Complex.

3. The readiness of the ignorant to trust "experts" unquestioningly regardless of how many times these very same people have been caught lying and misrepresenting medical and public health issues.

4. Total obliviousness and disregard of the human cost of these frauds

5. The moral cowardice of people who know better and keeps their heads down for personal comfort

The dishonesty of the news media has been thorough and complete.

Every half-baked, illogical, anti-scientific theory of doom is given screaming headline coverage with new ones being cooked up daily.

Here are the facts – the same facts that existed in March:

1. People without symptoms don't spread disease

2. The deaths that are taking place are occurring at about the same rate as a bad flu season

3. Deaths are overwhelmingly occurring among the frail elderly and people who have comorbidities (i.e. they are already sick with other serious illnesses.)

4. The young are not affected

5. As for every other outbreak like this in history, it has peaked – regardless of precautions taken – and is clearly fading away

The shutdowns, the mandated mask wearing, the testing of healthy people and tracing of their contacts, the hysteria to rush-develop a vaccine has been and continues to be medical fraud.

In countries with well-educated and relatively free people – Sweden, Finland, Denmark, the Netherlands, Slovenia – people have rejected mask wearing and yesterday there were mass protests in London and Berlin against them.

I doubt any of this is going to convince any of the True Believers.

Their egos are firmly entrenched in support of this charade and they're going to continue to smugly sit back and watch other people's lives ruined in the name of their Cause.

The CDC's fatal revised "CoVid fatality" numbers

September 03, 2020

You asked for the reference to the CDC's recent – and very quiet – revision of its "CoVid deaths" numbers.

First, three observations

1. You should ask for references about everything – especially when trillions of dollars and billions of lives are on the line.

It's strange that millions of people who "know the facts" didn't bother to check the facts – or got their facts from TV! – even when the intimate details of their own lives were at stake.

2. The CDC statement I cited yesterday should have been readily available to every person who has been affected by this thing.

Apparently, based on the volume of mail I'm receiving, a lot of people not only didn't see this all-important CDC statement reported anywhere in the news, they also can't find the relevant report on the CDC's website.

3. Why is the news media not reporting this, the most important statistic in the most important story in the world?

Your guess is as good as mine, though I suspect it has something to do with the fact that Pharma ads underwrite every TV news program and have now for many years.

Recap

To recap, because apparently the dementia epidemic is much broader than anyone realizes...

We were told SIX MONTHS AGO we had to shut down the world for two weeks, then fours week, then six weeks, then hell, until further notice, because there was a fatal, never-before-seen virus that is transmitted by people without symptoms and that there is no cure or treatment for it.

As I pointed out in yesterday's post, the Lead Medical Con Artist – and world's greatest expert on infectious diseases – Tony Fauci walked that back a little. It suddenly dawned on him – months into this – that people who don't have symptoms do not drive epidemics.

So scratch the "asymptomatic spreader" BS.

If you watch Fauci's videotaped admission, note how he skillfully shifts the blame to you for being "confused" about that point. Silly you.

OK, now, the fatal number – fatal to the fraud that is.

The exact quote buried deeply in the CDC's own fine print:

"Table 3 shows the types of health conditions and contributing causes mentioned in conjunction with deaths involving coronavirus disease 2019 (COVID-19).

For 6% of the deaths, COVID-19 was the only cause mentioned."

You can read the whole document here. It takes work to read it, which is why the conspirators are confident no one will do so.

https://www.cdc.gov/nchs/nvss/vsrr/covid_weekly/index.htm

What does it mean?

Of course, the number generated by the 6% will change as the total number of CoVid-RELATED cases increases.

If the total number of reported deaths is 150,000, then for the total number of deaths where the CDC now admits CoVid was the only factor, the number is 9,000.

If the total number of deaths is 160,000, then for the total number of deaths where the CDC now admits CoVid was the only factor, the number is 9,600.

The ever-shifting number is not the point.

The point is that the death numbers the media reports daily "from the CDC" are inflated by a factor of nearly 20 times. Not 20%, twenty times.

Just as Fauci finally admitted that asymptomatic spreaders have never before in the history of medicine been known to be epidemic spreaders of respiratory diseases, the CDC finally admitted what hundreds of thousands (millions?) of people have been saying for months:

"Dying WITH a disease among many others is not the same as dying OF a disease."

For example, if someone has dementia, diabetes, and heart disease and they catch a cold, no doctor who cares about protecting his license would dare attribute the patient's death to a cold.

Until the Age of CoVid Fraud.

Under the CoVid Con, all the normal standards of medicine, public health, and common sense have been thrown out the window.

In fact, doctors were ordered to change their standards for death reporting to specifically highlight CoVid regardless of other comorbidities, no matter how serious.

"Just call it CoVid and call it a day"... and most American doctors and public health officials complied.

The only other time in modern history I know of when there was such an extreme, systematized and officially sanctioned falsification of death records was during the Nazi era when German doctors were told to attribute the murder of inmates at forced labor camps to a variety of made up causes.

You can read all about it in Robert Jay Lifton's authoritative work on the subject "The Nazi Doctors." The specific references are here: pgs. 74-75, 100, 149, 187, 216.

So why are Fauci and the CDC going on the record with accurate information all of a sudden?

Here's my best guess: They're doing it so that when people eventually wake up – and I hope, for the sake of humanity, it's sooner rather than later – they can say: "But we told you all this!"

They know exactly what they're doing

Like the highly experienced bureaucratic weasels they are, they're setting the stage to shift the blame for the catastrophe to others, in this case "local officials."

All over the country, thousands of brain dead "officials" were empowered to do what they do best: 1) get endless free media time, 2) tell other people what to do, and 3) make exceptions for themselves and their friends, including industries well represented by lobbyists.

(See US Governors Andrew Cuomo, Gavin Newsom, Phil Murphy, and Gretchen Whitmer.)

Now, Fauci and Friends think they can use some verbal legerdemain to walk away scot-free from the carnage they created.

Here's what I'm guessing is their strategy. (Quotes mine)

"WE didn't tell them to do what they did. We don't have that kind of power and we'd never do that even if we could. We merely encouraged them to develop strategies to keep their communities safe. You can't blame us for what THEY did."

Either this is the best executed act of premeditated evil since Hitler and Friends rolled into Berlin or this is history's most pathetic demonstration of mental sloth, the elevation of the incompetent, and the nation's Mayberry Mussolinis losing their collective little minds with power.

Will Fauci and Friends get away with it?

Given the sad state of the news media, elected officials, academia, medicine, and I'm sorry to say the American people (huge organized protests in London and Berlin – nothing in the US), my guess is they'll not only get away with it, they'll get medals for their service.

Takeaway...

This may be hard to accept, but we're all mortal.

Everything we know and love, including our own lives, has an expiration date.

No politician, newscaster, public health bureaucrat or Pharma-co-opted MD is going to change that no matter how good their bullshit is.

Giving these people even one milligram of power more than they're legally or morally entitled to is a failing. They're literally among the least reliable members of society and the next time they open their mouths about anything, we should all remember that.

In the meantime, what matters is to build a good life with the life you've got.

Everyone able to read this has been given all the things needed to build a good life.

In the long run, the only thing that can interfere with us is foolishly falling for the connivance of evil people or behaving foolishly ourselves, two things under our complete control.

In short: take cheer.

These monsters can piss on everything they want, but they're mortal too and eventually they'll run out of piss and the rain will wash it all away like they were never here.

Meanwhile, let's use the brains and spines God gave us.

This is how bad things are

September 04, 2020

In 1963, John F. Kennedy went to Berlin to speak on behalf of freedom in front of an enormous crowd. Not only did the news media cover it then, it remains an iconic moment in modern history.

Last weekend, Robert F. Kennedy Jr, a lifelong environmental attorney, gave a talk to hundreds of thousands of people in Berlin who came out to protest the lock downs, the masks, and the entire "pandemic" medical fraud.

Not only did the so called "news" media not carry his comments, they reported the story as "Kennedy went to Berlin to speak to two or three thousand Nazi right-wingers."

When the news media lies this consistently and this massively, you don't need a PhD to know something is seriously, seriously wrong.

Kennedy lays out the case.

The pandemic is a fraud and I hope someday the people in my own country will have the intelligence and integrity to stand up for themselves the way the Germans are.

Here's my sincere plea to people who are standing on dry land, not starving, and have not lost their jobs and homes:

Get the cobwebs out of your head, grow a pair and stand up for the millions of innocent people who are being crushed by this non-stop fraud, and stop quietly enabling it.

But wait...there's more.

In between writing this page and queueing it for posting, a video came across my desk.

I verified it several different ways. It really happened.

Australian police entered the house of a family and handcuffed a pregnant woman in front of her small children for the "crime" of encouraging peaceful protest against the lockdowns with a post on Facebook, "inciting a riot", which is a criminal and jailable offense.

There's no shame in being temporarily fooled by government and news media con artists, but there does come a time when you have to ask: which side are you on?

But that's not all.

I just came across a news story from the NY Post. This woman, a nursing student, was arrested twice in front of New York City Hall for peacefully holding this sign. Her name is Linda Bouferguene.

It's worth making the effort to read her sign. She raised these basic questions in MAY and they still have not been addressed.

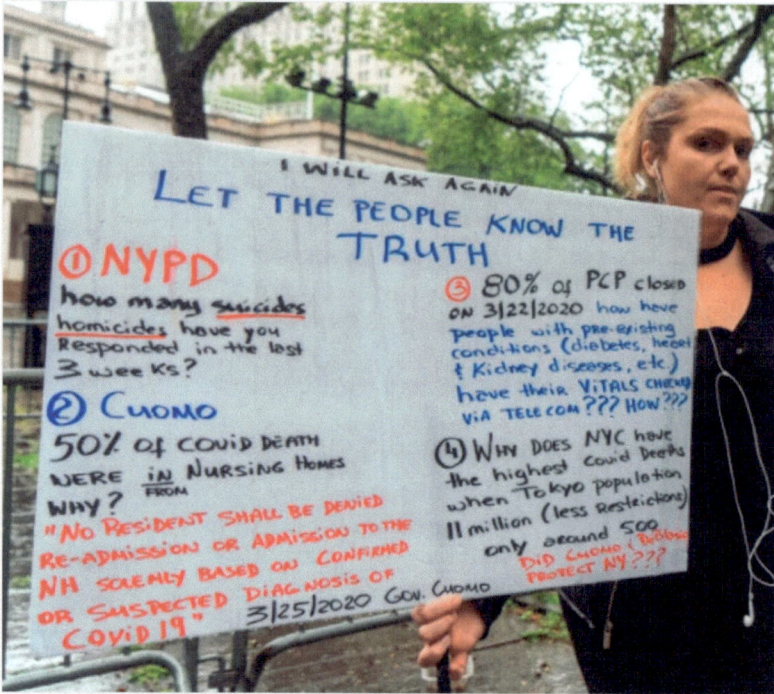

Linda Bouferguene

Something is very, very wrong. It has nothing to do with Right vs. Left, or Trump vs. Biden.

The normally unbalanced and unreliable people attracted to politics and government are behaving much more perversely than usual.

That's the issue and it's way past time for everyone to wake up and stop enabling the "killer virus" story.

Yes, the whole thing was illegal and the bureaucrats involved had no idea what they were doing

September 17, 2020

We've talked about the illogic of the locksdowns and business closures.

We've talked about the absurd Science 101 mistakes made by news media "experts" to justify the unjustifiable.

Now after hearing the testimony of Pennsylvania bureaucrats under oath – with lying being punishable under penalty of perjury – a federal judge has struck the whole thing down as "capricious and arbitrary" – and, most important, illegal.

You were not crazy. The world was crazy. Mentally lazy and heartless too.

So what do we do now?

Folks with well run direct response oriented businesses are doing fine. In fact, some are doing spectacularly.

I've been teaching the direct response method of doing business for the last 30 years and have generated many, many hundreds of hours of "how to" on this subject, the best of

97

which is available on tap for members of the System Club (http://www.thesystemclub.com/testdrive).

People who followed the principles laid out in the Independence Day Blueprint (available on Amazon) should be doing well too.

But there's more to this

Currently, I'm working with the largest non-profit social services agency in the region where I live – food, housing, and other essential things – to help them "up" their fundraising game as we head into what will surely be the biggest tidal wave of material misery this country has seen since the Great Depression.

I'd like to encourage readers to keep their eyes open for genuine grassroots groups where you live that are engineered to actually help people (vs. make jobs for bureaucrats.)

If there's interest, I'll share what I'm doing to help this group and you may be able to apply some of the lessons locally.

Fundraising is just another facet of marketing and anyone who can sell via direct response can be a first class fundraiser too. The skills are, for all practical purposes, identical and very few of the many worthy groups out there have even the first clue how to do it with maximum effectiveness.

Pay no attention to the man behind the curtain

October 04, 2020

It would take a book of many chapters to document the specific mechanics of how the CoVid Con was sold to the public, but it's knowable.

You need to know a little science and a little history and some technical but not complicated details of a "medical surveillance" and public relations infrastructure that's been under development at the hands of government bureaucrat careerists working in synch with the pharmaceutical industry since the 1950s.

If you read these books, you'll have the answer. I'll even flag some chapters for you.

- **Virus Mania** (2007) by Engelbrecht and Kohnlein MD (Especially Chapter 6)

- **False Alarm** (2005) by Marc Siegel MD (Especially Chapter 10)

- **Inventing the AIDS Virus** (1998) by Peter Duesberg, PhD. (Especially Chapter 3)

- **Crystallizing Public Opinion** (1923) by Edward Bernays

Bonus reading

- **The Nazi Doctors** (1986) Robert Jay Lifton MD (Especially Chapters 4 and 10)

- **The Search for an AIDS Vaccine** (1995) by Christine Grady. Christine Grady is Anthony Fauci's wife and current head of Ethics and Human Experimentation Standards for NIH.

Yes, you read that last bit correctly.

The news media is so braindead, corrupt and/or asleep at the switch they don't know that Tony Fauci's wife, through her job at NIH, rubber-stamps every drug and vaccine testing standard they violate here, in Africa and around the world.

What's going on is nothing less than the deliberate degradation of the Nuremberg Code. The Code was established after World War II in response to the demonic level of corruption that took place in medicine and medical science in Germany under the Nazi regime.

In Germany, the criminals were motivated by their allegiance to "Der Fuhrer." Among the Faucis and their many colleagues the driving force is their decades of allegiance to their corporate patrons, the pharmaceutical industry.

In case it's not blindingly obvious by now, this entire fraud was and is a scheme to market vaccines and other "therapies" by increasing product demand and making consumption mandatory by the deliberate and calculated misrepresentation of facts to terrorize the public.

Yes, there are people so sinister they'd cut your throat and the throats of your children and grandchildren just to make a buck, no doubt being True Believers in the sanctity of their "mission." Some of them wear suits and are routinely glorified by the news media.

Nurses and doctors in Europe say "No!"

October 20, 2020

I know a lot of people newly "educated" about biological science in the last few months think they're "following the science."

Uh, no. You're not.

You've been scammed and lied to non-stop since this whole farce began in Wuhan in 2019.

For starters, the PCR "test" – the one they're using to pump the CoVid fraud and scare people out of their minds – has never been anything more than a method to amplify small amounts of genetic material.

It was never meant to be a medical diagnostic tool. In fact, even the labels on the test kits confirm that.

There is no publicly available test that can show the SARS-2 virus in a blood sample.

All the PCR and other tests can do is recognize the presence of fragmentary genetic material that may or may not indicate the one-time presence of an active or inactive SARS-2 virus.

A positive test result does not mean you're sick.

It also does not mean you're infected with anything and it does not mean you're a "case."

So why are the news media anointed "experts" saying this?

Because the people running this thing are con artists.

How do I know?

The Nobel Prize winning INVENTOR of the PCR test said so.

Unfortunately, Kary Mullis passed away in the summer of 2019.

However, he left plenty of video behind.

He also left behind a book which in years past I sent to both Dan Kennedy and Perry Marshall because it's such a good read: Dancing Naked in the Mind Field (https://amzn.to/31qA3A7).

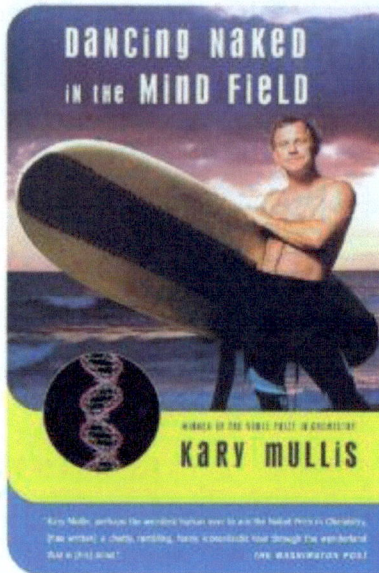

It does a great job of exposing the self-serving bullshit that "doctors" like Fauci and others have been serving up for decades.

For obvious reasons (he died before the current scam was hatched) we don't have Mullis' comments on CoVid, but we do have his comments on another Fauci scam.

The CoVid Con is following the same exact playbook that Fauci & Co used to turn AIDS "research" into a multi-hundred billion dollar money pump for themselves.

Thirty-six years later they still haven't delivered their promised vaccine and their "treatments" and "preventatives" cause more harm than the "disease" which, for most people, is just a positive test!

Fauci & Friends are not well intentioned "good guys" who just got a few things wrong.

They have a thirty-six year record of medical fraud and blood up to their elbows.

Nothing has changed

November 15, 2020

It's a bit tiring saying – and documenting – the same things over and over again (since March), but here goes:

1. Fauci & Co have been running near-identical frauds for decades. Unfortunately for us, they hit this one out of the park.

2. The idea of testing healthy, non-symptomatic people for anything is insane. Declaring people who have no symptoms "cases" or "infections" is insane. Quarantining people who've been "in contact" with non-symptomatic people – or merely traveled to a "suspect" state – until they get tested with the same unreliable tests is insane.

…But it is incredibly profitable for the testing companies that make $100 per go and the hospitals and medical groups that get emergency CoVid money every time they find a "new case."

3. Calling elderly people with one or more serious comorbidities who die in their 70s, 80s or 90s "killed by CoVid" based on a guesswork or technologically garbage testing is criminal.

4. Using this fraud as a justification for shutting down normal economic and social activity upon which the mental

and physical health of billions of people depends is a crime against humanity.

At this point, it's become equivalent to carrying out a holocaust, especially, but not only, in the developing world where unemployment means starvation and starvation guarantees illness and death.

5. Trump is an idiot for having allowed this to happen. His perpetuation of the "State of Emergency" and cheerleading for the rushed vaccine is a disgrace.

On the other side, Biden and Harris are so contemptible, they don't even merit comment.

People who are emotionally involved with either side have a screw loose.

For the elite few who can still think. You have my respect and affection.

Thank you.

Here's the deal...

I'm willing to go to Washington DC and march right now on this premise:

Get them ALL out – Trump, Biden, Pelosi, McConnell – the whole lot of them. And if we can find room in jail cells for them, all the better.

We're being "led" by the absolute dregs of humanity, and that includes the news media that's profiting from the endless oceans of bullshit they're spewing on an hourly basis.

There are numerous articles on this blog you can use to educate yourself about all this if you're so inclined.

It's long past time

November 19, 2020

Dr Roger Hodkinson, is the CEO of Western Medical Assessments, a company which sells CoVid-19 testing services.

Hodkinson received his general medical degrees from Cambridge University in the UK, and then became a Royal College certified pathologist in Canada (FRCPC) following a residency in Vancouver, BC.

He's the ex-President of the Pathology Section of the Canadian Medical Association and former Chairman of the Royal College of Physicians of Canada Examination Committee in Pathology.

He is eminently qualified to comment on the accuracy of the scientific reporting on CoVid, and he's called bullshit on all of it.

Finding videos of him speaking can be difficult, but if you search the uncensored video channels you'll find many.

Bottom line

People who have believed this fraud have been horribly deceived.

I don't blame anyone for being fooled.

The lying by government officials, public health bureaucrats, politicians and the news media has been unprecedented since the US was lied into Iraq and the citizens of New Orleans were blamed for the engineering failures of the U.S. Army Corps of Engineers.

That said, at this point, it is well past time to man and woman up, re-examine your position, and decide if you want your life record to include "I actively helped enable a medical fraud that caused serious injury to millions and millions of vulnerable people."

To err is human.

To persist in error is diabolical.

Nine months into this, given the seriousness of the situation and the number of people who are being devastated by it, we are deeply in diabolical territory.

There is no shame in having been deceived, but there is great dishonor in not thinking the issues through thoroughly after ample counter evidence has been presented and when the error is creating so much suffering.

Those of us who are standing on dry land and have the capacity to think and speak the truth are required to do so.

An honest mistake?

November 20, 2020

Once you realize that the Great Hysteria of 2020 is nothing more than a seasonal respiratory problem that's been dressed up as a deadly pandemic, the next logical question is:

Was this an honest mistake?

For the vast majority of people, yes, of course.

How many people have been to medical school or taken university level science courses? How many people have, and have read, over 100 books on biological science, medicine, and the history of medicine?

Not many. So, for a while, it's easy to fool people.

But as Abraham Lincoln reputedly said once:

You can fool all the people some of the time, and some of the people all the time, but you cannot fool all the people all the time.

I originally posted this video in the month of MAY.

https://www.youtube.com/watch?v=E1mivTZVI78

That's eight full months ago when the hysteria was relatively new and the confusion and trauma was fresh.

I wanted to take just one of dozens of fraudulent gambits being floated by the CDC, the NIH, the WHO, and their sinister enablers in the news media and put it under a microscope.

I could have easily done this full time, seven days a week, there were so many "CoVid" frauds being perpetrated (and there still are – daily.)

I am reposting the video again today (November 20, 2020) to make a point:

CoVid Hysteria was carefully and laboriously crafted with the expenditure of a great deal of time, money, thought and effort.

Most of the foot soldiers were simply "useful idiots", but make no mistake, the themes I analyze in this video were worked out and fed to the idiot news media by professionals.

Nothing you see on the TV news is spontaneous (unless it's an accident.)

It is all carefully scripted and produced as it needs to be. You can't very well get on live TV and "wing" it every night for an hour.

The problem – and it is a huge problem for our society – is when TV news producers act in a malevolent way.

Note: Any copywriter worth his or her salt should be able to instantly recognize how carefully these hysteria-pushing pieces were crafted and how fundamentally dishonest they were.

"Reporting" like this has been the norm for CoVid since day one.

This alone should have been a clue to the alert that something was seriously wrong with the integrity of the narrative.

By the way, it's 8 months later and none of the stories about children being at risk from CoVid turned out to have the slightest bit of truth to it.

Chapter 3

Second Thought: Lockdowns Indefinitely

Lockdowns are murder

November 28, 2020

"We in the World Health Organization do not advocate lock downs as a primary means of control of this virus... We may well have a doubling of world poverty by next year, we may well have at least a doubling of child malnutrition because children are not getting meals at school and their parents in poor families are not able to afford it. This is a terrible, ghastly global catastrophe actually. And so we really do appeal to all world leaders. Stop using lock down as your primary control method. Develop better systems for doing it, work together and learn from each other.

But remember, lock downs just have one consequence that you must never ever belittle. And that is: making poor people an awful lot poorer."   - David Nabarro

David Nabarro is Co-Director and Chair of Global Health at Imperial's Institute of Global Health Innovation, which he was appointed to in 2019.

In March 2020, David was appointed Special Envoy of WHO Director-General on COVID-19.

Somehow this clear statement by the WHO's top CoVid spokesman has been lost in the shuffle.

It just goes to show the dishonesty and depravity of the news media, the politicians, and the public health bureaucrats.

The news media is claiming that he is being "misquoted."

I can't imagine what the people who continue to advocate for these lockdowns are thinking:

1. The death rate from this thing is crystal clear now: It kills the same people who are killed by the flu, bad colds, and falls.

2. Mask wearing is biological idiocy: Viruses are many orders of magnitude smaller than the tightest masking material. All people are doing is increasing their chances of becoming sick from bacterial infections as the result of collecting and infecting themselves with the waste products of their lungs.

When in the history of science and medicine has inhaling a dirty rag for hours every day been considered a path to health?

3. Non-symptomatic (read that "healthy") people do not spread this (or any) disease as verified by a recent Chinese paper that failed to find one single case of "asymptomatic" spread in over 80,000 people studied.

4. The poor – people who actually work for a living as opposed to pushing paper, attending meetings and living off investments – are being massacred by this.

Nothing about any of this makes the slightest bit of sense.

This is a massive power grab and money pump based on fraud and the poor of the world are being savaged by it.

You think such calculated and depraved fraud is not possible?

The same thing happened just 10 years ago with the bird flu.

Amnesia is a very expensive societal self-indulgence.

The controlled demolition of small business in America

December 11, 2020

If we, the small business owners and small business advisors of the world, don't speak up for our colleagues, who is going to?

It is hard to interpret what is happening in many places in this country as anything other than a deliberate attack on small business owners, especially the restaurant and hospitality sector.

These folks provide employment, directly and indirectly, to tens of millions of people who otherwise don't have easy access to the jobs.

If the goal is to cripple this segment of our society and make them government dependents, they're right on track.

...They came for the trade unionists, and I did not speak out— because I was not a trade unionist.

Then they came for the Jews, and I did not speak out— because I was not a Jew.

Then they came for me—and there was no one left to speak for me.

– Martin Niemöller, Lutheran pastor imprisoned for seven years by the Nazis

We all better wake up and speak out – and fast.

Nothing about this story since the day it first started being reported in January is legitimate.

The endless variations of "containment" methods forced on the public are frauds based on systematic and deliberate misrepresentations of established science.

They might have made sense for a brief period in March – but even that is dubious. To continue them as they have been is a sinister joke.

Nothing has changed except some people's mindless tolerance for the situation.

Nature is resilient and so are you

December 12, 2020

Need I say more?

What ethical doctors are saying about the vaccine

January 18, 2021

What ethical doctors are saying about the masks, lockdowns and the vaccine.

First, an interview with Roger Hodkinson MD, chairman of the test committee in general pathology at the Royal College of Physicians and Surgeons of Canada, which sets the annual pathology board examination for Royal College.

Second, a well researched and thoroughly documented article on the nature of the vaccine written by a local MD I've known for twenty years.

But whether you are a doctor or a Ph.D. or not, it should be clear even to an illiterate that this whole thing was set up from Day One to be a massive payday for Pharma which now includes companies like Amazon, Google and, of course, Bill Gates and his various enterprises.

It's little reported that Google has billions of dollars invested in over one dozen Pharma ventures and that starting this past November Amazon went into head-to-head competition with pharmacies.

So you can see that this sick joke is on us.

Here's the medicine and science that the news media is doing its best to make sure you don't stumble across, PLUS an indication of just how hard the medical politicians are working to make sure you stay ignorant of their crimes.

#1 – Audio interview – System Club member Richard Jacobs interviews Roger Hodkinson MD of the Royal College of Physicians and Surgeons of Canada

https://www.findinggeniuspodcast.com/podcasts/politics-playing-medicine-a-closer-look-at-covid-19/

Or go to FindingGeniusPodcast.com and search Roger Hodkinson.

#2 – Article

Ronald D. Whitmont, M.D.
General Medicine-Homeopathy, P.C.
6250 Route 9
Rhinebeck, New York 12572
Phone: 845-876-6323
Fax: 845-876-2627

Dear Friends, Families and Colleagues!

There has been an incredible amount of information published recently on the current COVID-19 pandemic and I have spent months synthesizing as much as possible to present a coherent understanding of this virus. Every day new information appears. What follows is the most up-to-date information I could find. I apologize for the lengthy delay, as many of you have either written or called requesting guidance in this matter.Disclaimer: What follows is an extraction of a much larger paper that I hope to publish soon. This is NOT medical advice, nor it should not be taken as instruction about what to do.

The Bottom Line: I do not recommend either of the two available vaccines at this time, but everyone's health and susceptibility is different, and each person must make their own decision regarding whether the benefits of vaccination outweigh the risks for them, or not. At this stage, the vaccine has not been mandated, but there is a good chance that it will either be mandated, or that the social and societal pressures will become so great that for all intents and purposes it will be the same as a formal legal mandate. Only time will tell.

The COVID-19 pandemic itself is an example of how conventional medicine has insidiously destroyed the microbiome and weakened the immune system of an entire generation, making it more vulnerable to, among other things, a mutated respiratory virus. Not discussed in any forums: conventional treatments created the "perfect storm" of environmental, microbiome and immune system dysfunction that combined to weaken resistance and increase susceptibility to this virus. The "inconvenient truth" about conventional medicine, as important as it is in many conditions and circumstances, is that it is deadly harmful when overused, which is precisely what has been demonstrated by the current pandemic.

The immune system overreaction, aka cytokine storm, is believed to be the final common pathway leading to death from COVID-19, SARS, MERS and many other epidemic infectious diseases. This immune system hyper-reaction is more likely when the microbiome is disrupted (dysbiotic) and the immune system is dysfunctional: both common side effects of conventional medical treatment contributing to the risk of developing chronic inflammatory conditions, the comorbidities of COVID-19.

At least 24% of conventional medicines negatively impact the microbiome[1] leading to chronic dysbiosis and chronic inflammation. A host of chro᷈ ͜ inflammatory,[2],[3] autoimmune[4],[5] and neoplastic[6],[7] conditions plague modern societies using these drugs and Americans consume more of them, per capita, than any other country thus imparting the highest burden of chronic inflammatory disease anywhere in the world.[8],[9] Since comorbid chronic inflammatory diseases are risk factors that worsen outcome from COVID-19, and because Americans suffer from more of these conditions, and use more immune suppressing and microbiome damaging medications than the rest of the world, it shouldn't be surprising that US death rates from SARS-CoV-2 are among the highest.[10] According to the Journal of the American Medical Association (JAMA):

"the US has experienced more deaths from coronavirus disease 2019 (COVID-19) than any other country and has one of the highest cumulative per capita death rates.[11]

Data from the current worldwide COVID-19 pandemic provides direct evidence that the SARS-CoV-2 virus is only part of the problem (since 82% of people are already somewhat resistant to it) and that conventional medical treatments are what make a subset of the population more susceptible. Treatments that impair the immune system response and trigger rebound hyper-inflammation and immune cytokine storms are as responsible for complications as the coronavirus itself.[12]

Conventional medical care offers many powerful benefits and holds an important place in the management of many emergent, traumatic and surgical illnesses, but it appears to be largely ineffective and frequently harmful in the long-term management of many acute and chronic illnesses, particularly COVID-19. Interestingly, the COVID-19 pandemic does provide a very unique opportunity to understand some of the limitations of conventional medicine from a public health perspective.

Just like many other modern medical crises (antibiotic resistance, the opioid epidemic, and the epidemic of chronic inflammatory illness) the COVID-19 pandemic appears to be iatrogenic (caused by medicine or physicians). In other words, the current pandemic may be the indirect result of the overutilization of conventional allopathic medical treatments that damage the microbiome, the ecology of the environment and the immune system, resulting in greater susceptibility to this and a great many other illnesses.[13] Many conventional medical treatments increase susceptibility to comorbid conditions, as noted above, allowing the SARS-CoV-2 virus to act much more destructively.

Most of the comorbidities making COVID-19 more deadly are iatrogenic. These chronic inflammatory illnesses are overtly associated with 94% of all COVID deaths,[14] while the remaining deaths, in otherwise "healthy" individuals, are likely related either to a genetic predisposition or the overuse of conventional drugs (i.e., NSAID's and antipyretics) that are frequently used to manage symptoms of infection but increase the

128

odds of developing adverse events.[15] The overwhelming majority of healthy people (82%) suffer only mild or moderately from COVID-19, or not at all (45%).[16] Healthy young children have essentially a 0% risk of dying from COVID-19, while 93% of college age young adults,[17] 88% of pregnant women, and 96% of prisoners[18] appear to be completely immune, most never even developing symptoms from the virus.

The COVID-19 pandemic is not deadly in spite of conventional care; it appears to be deadly because of it.

Let me repeat that: The COVID-19 pandemic is not deadly in spite of conventional care; it appears to be deadly because of it. Many conventional treatments are associated with a dysfunctional immune-inflammatory response that contributes to a worsened outcome.[19] As late as October 2020, peer-reviewed guidelines in conventional medical journals indicated that "There are no [conventional medical] evidence-based treatments for COVID-19 that are appropriate for use,"[20],[21] but even worse, conventional treatments studied in clinical trials increase the risk of developing complications[22],[23] and the likelihood of dying or suffering from chronic post-COVID sequelae ("long COVID"),[24] which appears to result from "a dysfunctional immune-inflammatory response,"is precisely what conventional medications produce.[25]

The risk of developing an immune system hyperreaction (aka, a "cytokine storm" [26]) and dying from COVID-19 is much greater when conventional drugs are used, or if one already suffers from a chronic inflammatory comorbidity caused by or treated with conventional drugs.[27]

Many conventional medical treatments, which provide short-term symptomatic relief by suppressing the immune mediated inflammatory response, increase the risk of developing rebound uncontrolled hyper-inflammation, which leads toward a cytokine storm. Additionally, these drugs can block the connection between the innate and the adaptive immune systems, thus preventing the smooth transition to permanent adaptive immunity.[28] Further, many of these medications damage the microbiome[29] and dysregulate the immune system thereby increasing susceptibility to COVID-19 and other infections. It is no coincidence that these conventional medical interventions have not only proven to be inefficacious but are associated with an increased risk of death in pandemics.[30]

Many expect that a vaccine will stop COVID-19, but none of the vaccines currently in the pipeline have even been tested to find out if they will prevent infection from the SARS-CoV-2 virus.[31]

"None of the trials currently under way are designed to detect a reduction in any serious outcome such as hospital admissions, use of intensive care, or deaths. Nor are the vaccines being studied to determine whether they can interrupt transmission of the virus."[32]

Even manufacturers who boast a 90% or greater efficacy rate have not shown a reduction in symptomatic, asymptomatic, severe, or non-severe infections or burden of disease (BOD) since their primary endpoint in phase 3 clinical trials was only to prevent seroconversion. Clinical trials have not been completed, but FDA agreed to provide temporary emergency approval until they are (another 18 months at least.) The clinical trials required by the FDA for emergency approval only required "minimal phase 3 success criteria."[33] In other words, none of the vaccines were evaluated for risk or severity of illness, only the risk of testing positive for the virus. No determination has yet been made whether these vaccines will prevent illness or transmission, reduce complications or prevent death above or beyond placebo treatment.

Experts at the British Medical Journal (BMJ) raised serious concerns that many cases of illness following vaccination, not testing positive for COVID-19, were excluded from the study, skewing the results in favor of the vaccines, when these may have been serologic negative cases and evidence of vaccine failure.[34]

These vaccines were rushed to market without any form of FDA site inspection,[35] even as widespread reports described the emergence new mutations in the SARS-CoV-2 virus. No clinical trial has addressed whether new mutations will even affect vaccine efficacy or not (perhaps because the true efficacy will not be known until trials are completed in another 18 months). As all viruses mutate, which SARS-CoV-2 has already done many times, and will continue to do, there is a known tendency to become less lethal and more benign with each subsequent adaptation.[36] Viruses are under constant evolutionary pressure, not only to advance from one species to another, but to adapt benignly to their hosts and develop a commensal relationship that increases longevity of both species.

This ability to constantly mutate and adapt increases the risk that vaccines, if they are not produced fast enough, will be obsolete before they can be administered. This is precisely why the Cuban Ministry of Health approved the emergency use of a homeopathic immunization in 2007 against epidemic leptospirosis. Not only was the campaign effective in preventing disease, but the homeopathic product was produced rapidly, safely and inexpensively and was distributed to over 2.5 million people in a short period of time.[37] This type of program is a model of rapid targeting, development and deployment using a safe and effective modality to effectively prevents and treat illness without imposing new risks of harm. It was an example that probably terrified the modern vaccine industry since the product did not utilize advanced technology, could not be patented and did not generate billions of dollars in revenue.

As vaccination against other epidemic diseases, like influenza, has clearly demonstrated: most vaccines don't work well in the elderly or infirm populations,[38] which is precisely the demographic at highest risk from COVID-19. It is unlikely that vaccines will generate immunity in this population without multiple doses, which may significantly increase the risk of allergic reactions.

Additionally, since 82% of the untreated population is already relatively immune from serious adverse reactions to the SARS-CoV-2 virus, and the vaccine may not even prevent transmission, it is likely those who are most vulnerable will continue to be so. Even if the vaccine does generate an immune response, no vaccine has ever been associated with durable permanent immunity, or even come close to the long-lasting immunity produced by actual infection, which is "substantial" and durable in the case of COVID-19.[39],[40]

Since immunity from all vaccines inevitably wanes with time, future waves of this and other viruses in a vaccinated population are still likely to be costly and damaging. This phenomenon has already been demonstrated by many current childhood vaccination programs: as the vaccinated population ages and immunity wanes, childhood diseases become more devastating if it is contracted by those who are older.[41] If natural illness and the resulting long-term or permanent immunity is allowed to develop, then protection tends to be more durable.

An important consideration is that the existing program of overusing vaccines to prevent routine infections in the US may be one of the factors already contributing to the excess death rate from COVID-19. The US vaccine schedule is heavier than those in any other country and many of these vaccines are associated with increased risk of chronic illness[42] while others, like the influenza vaccine, are known to increase susceptibility to a wide range of acute infections, including coronaviruses.[43] Interestingly, health care workers are some of the most heavily vaccinated adults in the US, and they appear to be extremely susceptible to complications from the SARS-CoV-2 virus,[44] suggesting a link between vaccination and immune system susceptibility.[45]

All of the vaccines currently approved for use against COVID-19 in the US utilize a relatively new (mRNA) technology designed to provoke protein synthesis by genetically modifying existing cellular machinery in a fashion similar to the way that real viruses act. Preliminary testing of coronavirus vaccines for SARS-CoV infections revealed that both vaccine hypersensitivity reactions as well as adverse histopathologic lung changes can occur in vaccinated individuals, increasing the risk of greater disease severity and death in those who subsequently encountered either the actual virus or a vaccine re-challenge,[46] leading researchers to suggest that:

"Caution in proceeding to application of a SARS-CoV vaccine in humans is indicated."[47]

The COVID-19 vaccines are essentially man-made "Frankenviruses" that use a lipid nanoparticle membrane bound together by a synthetic adjuvant, polyethylene glycol (PEG), a relative of ethylene glycol (the main poisonous ingredient in automobile

134

antifreeze[48]) instead of a phospholipid or protein coat that surrounds most natural viruses:

"The main difference between ethylene glycol and polyethylene glycol is that ethylene glycol has a fixed value for molecular weight whereas polyethylene glycol has no fixed value for molecular weight."[49]

PEG has never been utilized in a vaccine before, but it is so far, associated with a 24-fold increased risk of severe allergic reactions (anaphylaxis) already seen in many COVID-19 vaccine recipients.[50]

The COVID-19 vaccines, once injected, indiscriminately bind to and "infect" random human cells, hijacking the protein synthesis machinery and forcing then to produce viral proteins until the mRNA is degraded. These vaccines mimic the way actual viruses behave, but unlike natural viruses that bind only to specific receptors in certain cells, these man-made viruses have the potential to take control of any cell including those in the vital organs like the heart, liver, kidneys or eyes, which would then become a target of the immune system. Training the immune system to react to any of these vital tissues could lead to catastrophic long-term side effects that may not be evident until many months or years later.

Since genetic and chemical information is continually traded and shared between virtually all cells within the human organism and the human microbiome as part of a complex messaging system,[51] genetically engineered information can enter this pool with unforeseen, unintentional and unstudied side effects.

Incorporating genetically engineered information into other species of bacteria and viruses in the human microbiome and virome[52] could create a de novo genetic breeding program similar to what is seen when antibiotics select resistant organisms or "super bugs" that share or trade genetic information for resistance. Monkeying with the genome with this heretofore untested and unproven technology may open up an entirely new and unprecedented frontier of medical terrorism by creating new genetically modified organisms (GMO's) capable of affecting the body in unforeseen ways, entering the microbiome and dispersing freely in the environment. This unregulated trial without adequate safety studies is reminiscent of other failed experiments that have led to other environmental and health disasters. Safety testing is not an area that can or should be skipped or overlooked since these changes can have long lasting ramifications with unknown and unpredictable consequences across the entire ecosystem, not restricted to their intended use. Just like "Silent Spring:"

"We stand now where two roads diverge...The road we have long been traveling is deceptively easy, a smooth superhighway on which we progress with great speed, but at its end lies disaster." [53]

No one knows exactly what the long-term effects on the microbiome, the environment or the human immune system will develop from these vaccines

136

because they have been fast-tracked without time to consider either short or long-term safety and efficacy.[54]

Additionally, after spending billions of dollars to rapidly develop several COVID-19 vaccines at "warp speed," the world is facing an unprecedented ethical dilemma: will otherwise healthy people, at low risk of illness be directly mandated or indirectly pressured to take an unproven, untested medical product that even the US supreme court ruled in 2010 in BRUESEWITZ ET AL. v. WYETH LLC, FKA WYETH, INC., ET AL., to be "unavoidably unsafe"? [55]

Vaccinating otherwise healthy individuals, already at low risk of complications from COVID-19, with an untested, unproven vaccine capable of inducing significant environmental and immune system havoc is inadvisable, unnecessary and reckless. This not only increases risk of exposure to chemicals, toxins, adjuvants,[56] viral and genetic contaminants in the vaccines,[57], [58] but increases the risk of promoting chronic immune stimulation and hyperinflammation,[59] particularly in women who are more susceptible.[60] Mandating this vaccine for everyone, including healthy people, rather than offering it to those at highest risk, would be a mistake, a gross corruption of the democratic process, a violation of the Nuremburg Codes[61] and a flagrant violation and neglect of the principles of "informed consent."[62]

The COVID-19 pandemic desperately begs to be studied in relation to the long-term effects of using conventional allopathic medicines and vaccines. Failure to heed these connections, or to explore the relationship between what preceded this pandemic and what follows, may mean the difference between environmentally based health and man-made provoked chronic illness. Pandemics may become more prolonged and commonplace as environmental and microbiome destruction, mass extinctions, and climate changes accelerate under this pernicious system.

The vaccine decision is not an easy one. Many scientific and ethical questions remain unaddressed and unanswered.

Thank you!

Sincerely,

Ronald D. Whitmont, MD

The "Why"

January 31, 2021

A business and marketing advisor I respect a great deal recently gave advice to his subscribers regarding the Scamdemic and other government and Big Business atrocities.

His recommendation? "Keep your head down."

The vast majority of marketing advisors seem to be following this course.

Obviously, I have taken a different approach to this matter.

I'm not interested in politics. If I want to be entertained by the antics of deranged criminals I'll watch "The Godfather" or "Scarface."

On the other hand, we don't live separate from society. We are, for better or worse, embedded in it and there are some issues where silence is not an option – for me at least.

I'm not telling anyone else what to do. There are potential consequences for sticking one's head up and some people are better positioned to weather them than others.

That said, it's worth at least considering taking a stand.

It may indeed cost you customers and bring heat down on you and neither of these are trivial matters. On the other hand, in case you've lost sight of this, you're not going to live forever or in perfect comfort no matter how self protective you are.

Anyway...

Robert F. Kennedy Jr. started his career as an environmental attorney and through that experience he learned about devastating effects of mercury on the human body, especially children.

This led him to found Children's Health Defense to protect children and others from abuses by the government and the pharmaceutical and medical industries.

As an intelligent man who saw both his uncle and his father murdered for political reasons (don't even dream "lone nut" assassins were the only ones involved), he has a unique perspective on the various forces at play in American society and how they've come together in this most sinister and demented scam.

As I've said since the very beginning, this whole thing is a COMMERCIAL enterprise.

They want to sell more vaccines. Beginning, middle, and end of story. It's hard for me to imagine how anyone without organic brain damage fails to grasp this at this point.

As Kennedy pointed out (as I did ten months ago), Gates has been working on this goal nonstop for over ten years and has spent literally billions of dollars to pave the way, buying effective control of news media outlets and national and international health agencies.

This is not a conspiracy theory.

The amounts Gates has spent and who he has spent them on are a matter of public record. You might be surprised to learn that in addition to billions given to the CDC and the WHO, he's spent over $100 million dollars in direct grants in the last two years alone to Reuters, NPR, the Los Angeles Times, the Washington Post, Le Monde in France, El Pais in Spain, and dozens of other "news" outlets all over the world.

But there's more.

They're not only trying to expand the vaccine franchise, they are desperately trying to save the one they've got.

Bottom line: No reasonably healthy person should ever die of a viral disease. (The very frail elderly and those with serious advanced medical conditions are a different story. We're mortal. We die. Get over it.)

The pharmaceutical cartel and the people who support it are vicious.

They will literally let you and your loved ones die in order to suppress the reality that there are safe, effective and inexpensive medicines that make their expensive and dangerous products completely unnecessary.

As I laid out in an interview by Perry Marshall in April, "CoVid" is the coming together of the interests of the most depraved elements of society – Pharma, Big Tech, Wall Street, the Defense industry, the news media and the deviants attracted to local and national government.

They all believe they have something massive to gain from a brutal regimentation of society and they're pushing hard – together – to achieve their aims.

I recommend you don't support them.

Ethical doctors being harassed for not participating in the CoVid Con

February 4, 2021

Sam Bailey MD is a licensed physician in New Zealand.

She has been posting videos to YouTube since 2017 and has had over 12,000,000 views of her well researched, well documented and well produced videos.

Bailey is representative of the small percentage (less than 1%) of physicians who've been publicly calling BS on the various CoVid frauds.

Doctors who take these kinds of public stands are routinely harassed and threatened with losing their licenses.

If there are heroes in this ongoing travesty, *they* are among them, and they need our support.

If you've had basic questions about the situation we find ourselves in, she consistently presents the most thorough and comprehensive answers.

You can find her videos on Odysee.com. Like so many ethical doctors and scientists she's had her work removed by Google/Youtube.

"Not a single thing the authorities said was true."

April 06, 2021

Google/YouTube has removed dozens of my videos.

People, including me, who've shared similar information have had their Twitter accounts frozen.

I have trouble understanding how people think they're going to survive and thrive in the real world, let alone be seen as legitimate advisors to others when they can't see through – and won't stand up to – a blatant and obvious fraud that has actively harmed hundreds of millions of people.

In marketing, there's the message and then there's the INFRASTRUCTURE to deliver the message.

If you're wondering how the conspirators pulled off this epic masterpiece of fraud, you need to know about the infrastructure.

As far as I know, the only place you're going to get insight into this is here. It will take a little time, but if you want to know the nature of the world you're in, there are no shortcuts. The alternative is to be a voluntary dupe.

How to sell a vaccine (or other "solution" to a public health problem)

1. Claim the emergence of a new and deadly virus that no one has immunity to – even if it's not true

2. Claim it spreads easily and that every living person regardless of age and health status is at risk – even if it's not true

3. Claim that there are no effective treatments for the problem – even if it's not true

4. Use these claims to put people into a fear and panic state

5. Use this state to create society-crippling restrictions with the false claim that they represent science

6. Claim to have a new technology that greatly speeds up the vaccine development process

7. State that the world can't go back to normal until "the entire global population is vaccinated" (Bill Gates pronouncement in March of 2020)

8. Use the above aforementioned frauds to distribute a vaccine under "Emergency Use Authorization" obscuring the fact that the vaccine has not been approved for use on human beings by the FDA and cannot, based on long accepted safety testing practices, until 2023

9. Weaponize the scum of the earth – politicians, news media hacks, political ideologues, unthinking morons who make pronouncements that affect others without knowing the first thing about what they are talking

about – to push for everyone to accept the story and the product, in this case, a vaccine, and along with it a medical philosophy that is a complete departure from well established and effective medical practices pre-2020.

The massive network designed to hype "epidemics." It's been place – and growing – for over 60 years

Fauci's track record is as a self-serving medical con artist.

The Good Doctors

April 25, 2021

There are good doctors.

They are rare.

So what's going on?

Why is a safe, inexpensive, effective remedy for CoVid being suppressed in the United States?

The answer to this question is the serious and widespread moral cowardice of doctors in this country.

Many doctors – perhaps the majority now – believe it is better to use "approved" methods that don't work and watch you become unnecessarily sick, disabled, or even die, than it is for them to put their personal money-making machine, their MD license, at-risk and actually practice medicine.

Yes, it's that bad.

This was a serious problem long before the CoVid Con debacle.

Now the whole corrupt, dysfunctional system is being exposed for what it is.

Based on my own experiences, I've long told my System Club members that if you have a severe medical problem, you better become the expert on it and research like you've never researched in your life.

You absolutely cannot count on the typical doctor today to: a) be up on current research, b) be aware of effective treatments that don't cost an arm and a leg, or c) give you informed, unbiased advice.

Fortunately, there are some doctors who don't follow the party line and put their patient's health and success first, above all.

However, they are not the norm. You have to hunt for them.

Understand this: The various vaccines being pushed have not been approved by the FDA. They are YEARS away from passing their safety tests.

They are being distributed and administered based on Emergency Use Authorization (EUA).

The standards for Emergency Use Authorization are: a) there is a grave, new public health risk and b) there is no known treatment.

Simply declaring these two things, whether they are true or not, is all it takes for ANYTHING to be "approved" under EUA.

The suppression of safe, effective treatments for CoVid-19 creates the justification for the distribution of vaccines that have been rushed to market and are based on theories and technology that are far from proven.

Everything I've said here – the fact the FDA has not approved these vaccines and that they are being distributed under EUA – can be verified on the FDA's own website.

If your doctor, your local "leaders", and the news media don't know this they're incompetent.

If they do, they're knowingly participating in a criminal enterprise that has resulted in the deaths and needless suffering of countless thousands of people.

All so a few pharmaceutical companies can show a good quarter.

That's what this is about.

That's what this has been about since March of 2020 when Bill Gates declared we needed a vaccine and that the world can't get back to normal until it's developed and everyone gets it...for a disease that only impacts the already sick and can be treated safely for a few bucks.

This has been and remains one of the most sinister con jobs in human history.

A crime against humanity based on fraud

May 06, 2021

The false narrative behind the fear and panic

- A deadly novel virus is sweeping the planet

- Nobody is immune and there is no cure

- Asymptomatic people are major drivers of disease

- So we have to lock down and wear masks until everyone is vaccinated

- Anyone who challenges this narrative is a danger to society

Nothing would make me happier than to stop writing on this subject…

…But whether it makes "good business sense" or not I'm not going to stop until this thing has a stake driven through its heart.

Those of us who care must all do our parts to inform those who still have a brain left in their heads – a shockingly small number of people – as to what is going on and why it's completely unacceptable.

150

A happy story

May 15, 2021

A school administrator with integrity.

No masks, no plexiglass, no social distancing.

In short, no BS.

Intelligence. Decency. Courage.

So rare, but people like this do exist.

FACT: The injectable products being sold as "CoVid vaccines" are NOT approved by the FDA for use on human beings.

They are being distributed under Emergency Use Authorization which is most definitely NOT the same thing as FDA approval. You can confirm this by reading – carefully reading – the FDA's own statement on its website.

If you want to participate as an unpaid test subject, have at it. It's a free country, but at least be informed about what you are agreeing to.

There's one school administrator in Florida who's not having it.

If you've never read the Nuremberg Code, here's the first paragraph (highlights mine.)

*"The voluntary consent of the human subject is absolutely essential. This means that the person involved should have legal capacity to give consent; should be so situated as to be able to exercise free power of choice, **without the intervention of any element of force, fraud, deceit, duress, overreaching, or other ulterior form of constraint or coercion**; and should have sufficient knowledge and comprehension of the elements of the subject matter involved as to enable him to make an understanding and enlightened decision. This latter element requires that before the acceptance of an affirmative decision by the experimental subject **there should be made known to him the nature, duration, and purpose of the experiment; the method and means by which it is to be conducted; all inconveniences and hazards reasonably to be expected; and the effects upon his health or person which may possibly come from his participation in the experiment."***

Following WWII, Nazi doctors were hung for subjecting human beings to medical experiments without proper consent.

Gates, Fauci and all their hired hands have done a first class job of stampeding the gullible into volunteering for what no one in their right mind would normally do:

Accepting a rushed, experimental therapy not approved by the FDA for a disease you don't have and one that if you do get has an extremely low probability of causing you any serious harm.

Finally, it's just one anecdote, but it's close to home. A neighbor recently told me his uncle "died of CoVid" - the week after he got the vaccination. 90% of people who hear stories like this will just shrug their shoulders without any independent thought at all. I hope you're not one of them.

Survival in spite of the government

July 19, 2021

You have to laugh every time a politician gets on TV and talks about how much he or she is doing for small business. The reality is there is no more destructive or harassing force small business people face than the government.

Last year, around this time, we posted a video from a restaurateur friend Charlotta Janssen about a neighborhood of restaurants that were in danger of being driven out of business...

Not by the "pandemic", but by government ineptitude and mindless viciousness.

In order to boost real estate values for large-scale developers, the local government banned outdoor dining, effectively killing the last hope these small businesses had for survival.

Here's the good news.

By getting together and with the support of some people on this list – you know who you are – they organized, forced sanity on their local scum politicians, and survived against all odds.

Now, Round Two.

Sometimes success – or even survival – in business depends on such things.

Bait and Switch

September 01, 2021

The current "standard of care" is that when people test positive and have symptoms to send them home with no treatment whatsoever and deal with them later in an emergency room if they come down with an advanced case

In other words, business as usual for "modern" medicine.

If this approach sounds ignorant and sinister, you are thinking clearly and perceiving the situation accurately.

When you combine science with politics – you get politics

How is it possible that young otherwise healthy people in Israel are ending up in the ICU AFTER getting their "magic" vaccine?

The political answer is "the variant" and the apparent failure of people to "understand" that the "magic" vaccine wears out after a few months (in contrast with natural immunity which lasts for life.)

It's called "bait and switch."

You're sold one thing and then given another and that's what "CoVid" has been about since Day One.

Examples:

- "We need to shut down for two weeks to protect the hospitals."

– Over 18 months later, lockdown-type restrictions are still in play all over the world including many places in the U.S.

- "Just wear the masks for a little while. They'll stop the spread."

– Masks were well known not to suppress the spread of disease long before COVID and have proven to be ineffective and unhealthy during COVID, but are now a daily reality for millions – 18 months after "a little while."

- "Get the vaccine. It's safe and effective and our only way out."

– Israel is telling the truth. They're covering it in BS, but telling the truth. The vaccine does not work. Period.

Now the reality which Bill Gates and others spelled out at the beginning of all this and actually spent decades preparing the way for:

You are being set up to be required to get vaccine after vaccine and provide proof of vaccination or you will be locked out of normal society (employment, going to school, eating in restaurants, attending live entertainment, staying in hotels, flying in airplanes etc.)

Facts about COVID

1. The death rate was wildly exaggerated

2. The transmissibility rate was wildly exaggerated

3. The people specifically at risk for a bad outcome was wildly exaggerated

4. It was a treatable disease almost from day one

5. The fact that is successfully treatable in its early stages was and continues to be savagely repressed

The autopsies

If you have a loved one who dies immediately after a COVID vaccination, you will be told: "It was their time." (In contrast, if they're 90 years old with stage four cancer and dementia you'll be told: "They died of COVID.")

Some people are not buying this bullshit. They're paying for autopsies when "public health officials" decline.

We now know the "99.9% effective" was bullshit (how could anyone over the mental age of five have not seen through that?) and now it's shaping up that these vaccines are not safe either.

The same people have done this before

If you haven't seen "Fauci's First Fraud" yet, you really should. CoVid is a replay of another sinister scam Fauci and Friends ran 40 years ago.

The fact that it was allowed to stand – and is still believed by millions – is the reason we are where we are today.

A ray of CoVid sanity

October 01, 2021

Two of the best-managed and least corrupt countries in the world that take exponentially better care of their citizens' health than the U.S – Norway and Singapore – have declared CoVid Hysteria is over within their borders.

They're done. Finished. Their official policy is "we're going to live with it like we live with the flu." Sane public education on the matter will replace the mass media hysteria.

No more ever-changing mandates. No mandatory vaccinations. No vaccine passports. No masking of kids. (The last one is easy. Europe NEVER masked their kids.)

The era of self-inflicted harm caused by legions of ignorant hypochondriacs is over – for them at least.

How long will the spiteful, moronic, politicized "public health policy" of the U.S. and other corrupt, abusive governments like Canada's and Australia's continue?

We'll see.

Meanwhile, it's amazing that our "news" media has managed to keep these two plain vanilla CoVid news stories off their front pages and from the evening news, isn't it? Spread the word. Your family and friends will never see this news on TV.

Remember science?

October 03, 2021

"You're a lawyer with no scientific background": Rand Paul attacks Sec. Becerra on vaccine mandates.

U.S. Senator Rand Paul calls out Xavier Becerra, the head of the Department of Health and Human Services (HHS).

Becerra is an attorney and politician and has absolutely no background in science or medicine – yet he somehow has achieved dictatorial power over the health decisions of individuals and businesses in the U.S.

Employ over 100 people? You are required to demand they all be vaccinated or receive a $750,000 fine.

Want your children to be educated? You better line them up for a vaccine.

As California's Attorney General under Gavin Newsom, Becerra enabled some of the most unhinged and destructive lockdowns in the U.S.

But that's not all.

In December 2020, California state district attorneys formally complained that he was doing nothing to help stop unemployment fraud during the COVID-19 pandemic, in what was described as the "biggest taxpayer fraud in California history". In January 2021, investigators said the total fraud was over $11 billion, with $19 billion in claims still under investigation. Prosecutors said they believe that because of Becerra's inaction most of this money will never be recovered.

But this is a much bigger issue than one corrupt, arrogant political operative.

Virtually nothing we were told about CoVid-19 – and which tens of millions of people still believe – turns out to be true.

Its transmissibility; its fatality rate; who is and is not at risk from a catastrophic outcome; the existence of safe, inexpensive, and effective therapies – all of the "information" from authorities and the news media has proven to be false.

Yes, people died of respiratory illness. They die of cancer, heart disease, diabetes and old age too by the millions every year. Welcome to Real World 101.

The officially recommended prevention methods have equally been proven to be false.

Heavily promoted hand sanitizing gels, many of which contain toxins, are less effective than simple alcohol-based products and plain soap and water by the CDC's own fine print admission.

Masks, especially "make-believe" cloth masks and flimsy surgical masks intended to protect patients undergoing surgery from contamination from doctors and nurses in the operating room, have long been well known to be pointless in preventing the spread of respiratory diseases yet were – and in some places still are forced on people including children – for 8 or more hours per day.

There was science and medicine before 2020 – and it was all thrown out the window to sell the CoVid Panic.

And the purpose of selling CoVid Panic?

To sell vaccines. Period.

At least 100,000,000 Americans do not need this product. They had CoVid and have natural immunity exponentially superior to the "95% effective" vaccine that has already broken down so thoroughly it already requires booster shots.

That's the science.

Remember that? "Follow the science."

"The science" only appears to matter when it supports selling vaccines.

So why the manic push to vaccinate everyone, especially when "cases" (in fact nothing more than positive test results) are declining and we're at or very close to herd immunity?

Above and beyond the desire of the power-mad to control others down to the last detail of their lives, there's an economic twist to this story you probably won't hear anywhere else.

The vaccines have a shelf life of about 9 months.

What happens to a vaccine that does not "go into arms" and expires?

At midnight, Cinderella-like it turns from a coach to a pumpkin, from a profit center to an expense.

It costs real money to safely and legally dispose of expired vaccines. Expired vaccines are, quite rightly, categorized as medical waste and their handling is highly regulated and expensive.

The vaccines started their initial rollout in December 2020 and there have been successive waves of manufacturing since. The makers and distributors are sitting on huge inventories.

Look at the calendar. This latest wave of hysteria is right on schedule, nine months after the vaccines started rolling out of the factories.

The vaccines are expiring. The people who stage-managed this fraud from day one know it. They need to get them into as many arms as possible or they will have to pay to dispose of them.

Forcing employers to betray their employees...stampeding parents into betraying their children...and if there are any vaccines leftover, they'll have the taxpayers pay to put them in the arms of random people in poor countries just as they've done with previous vaccine marketing campaigns.

Create the demand, sell like mad and don't stop until every last piece of inventory is profitably off the shelves...

All socially engineered as anyone who knows anything about marketing should be able to see through by now.

How we end this now

November 06, 2021

Question: Should science be censored so politicians, bureaucrats and the social engineers who fund them can advance their pet agendas?

Apparently, Google, Facebook, Twitter, Instagram, NBC, CBS, ABC, CNN, FOX, Mark Zuckerberg, Bill Gates and the White House and federal governments around the world seem to think so.

What do you think?

Sometimes there's only one way to go through an impenetrable brick wall – around it. And **your help is urgently needed** right now to do just that.

The last bastion of uncensored speech in America is found between the covers of books and the places people find them: libraries, bookstores, even the bestseller list of the otherwise corrupt New York Times.

Thus, our project: The marketing of a book – *The Real Anthony Fauci* by Robert F. Kennedy Jr. – which has all the data and history you and millions of others have been denied the last 18+ months.

There are already 52,000+ pre-launch cash-with-order sales on Amazon, but we're a little weak at the local independent store level, which is critical for making it to the NYT bestseller list...

And it's why I'm writing to you today to ask for your help.

Once on the New York Times bestseller list, the much-censored information in this book will, at last, be out of the dark, but we're not going to get there on luck. It's going to take concerted action.

Do you have a list? What can you do to help?

1. Let your people know that they can get an authoritative answer to "What's going on?" in this book.

2. Also, if they want to be part of stopping this madness, they need to get to their local bookstore and order at least one copy, though preferably more for friends and family, THIS WEEKEND.

3. If you can manage nothing else today, there is a link below to purchase a copy from Amazon.

P.S. I'm interested in hearing from anyone with a sizable list or lists who want to be part of this. Time is of the essence. Thanks.

P.P.S. If you can do nothing else, hit the link and buy one or more copies from Amazon.

The Real
Anthony
Fauci

Bill Gates, Big Pharma, and
the Global War on Democracy
and Public Health

Robert F. Kennedy Jr.
NEW YORK TIMES BESTSELLING AUTHOR

Children's
Health Defense

How we'll win

November 13, 2021

Books...They can't be deleted, canceled, or have their accounts closed.

They don't get lost on hard drives, they don't require batteries to operate, and you can easily share them.

As you read this, we are within a hair's breadth of getting Robert F. Kennedy Jr's scathing exposure of Anthony Fauci's multi-decade career of crimes against humanity (**"The Real Anthony Fauci"**) onto the New York Times bestseller list – all in the face of a total news media blackout.

At times, we've been the #1 pure-play (non-memoir, non-self help) non-fiction bestseller on Amazon.

Now is crunch time. The book formally launches on November 16.

You have been selected... to be a freaking hero.

If you are one of the legions of decent people who want to do something about this self-inflicted catastrophe on humanity, I know of no better thing you can do right now than support this book by buying one or more copies **this weekend**.

As an incentive to PWMs (if you are one, you know what it means), buy this book in quantity, send me your receipt, and I'll send you the following:

* Five copies or more

My exclusive no-holds-barred interview with Dan Kennedy in which we get into topics he has never shared with any audience before.

Until now, this treasure, like my interview with Gary Bencivenga, was for members of the System Club only. I'm opening it up this one time for this cause only.

I've been Dan's student for 32 very profitable years and a colleague for almost as long. You're highly unlikely to ever come across this deep of a dive into his work from any other source.

* Ten copies or more

The above plus...

Access to the ultimate GOAT seminar on the secret inner dynamics of writing successful direct response ad copy.

The recording of the full all-day seminar with me, Perry Marshall, and Drayton Bird. This is the only time the three of us got together to offer a training and it will never be repeated.

Perry is, of course, the author of the bestselling Internet marketing book of all time.

Drayton is the UK's most distinguished direct response marketer, with over 50 years of experience under his belt. His direct response agency was so strong in the UK, the only way David Ogilvy could crack the market was to buy them out.

I, of course, am the GOAT who first brought direct response and Internet marketing together and changed the world as we know it in the process.

Let's buy some books!

https://thefaucibook.com/order-options/

DEADLINE: Monday, November 15, 2021 midnight eastern standard time. No exceptions.

Called it, did it

November 19, 2021

Amazon Best Sellers
November 19, 2021
8:26 AM Eastern

Our most popular products based on sales. Updated hourly.

Best Sellers in Books

#1 — The Real Anthony Fauci: Bill Gates, Big... › Robert F. Kennedy Jr. ★★★★★ 139 — Hardcover $17.59

#2 — The 1619 Project: A New Origin Story › Nikole Hannah-Jones ★★★★½ 49 — Hardcover $24.33

#3 — All American Christmas › Rachel Campos-Duffy ★★★★½ 32 — Hardcover $18.77

In March of 2020, I told you Fauci was not straight.

Since then, I've devoted a lot of my blog to documenting the details.

Why did I do this?

- I don't want to see small businesses and whole communities destroyed

- I don't want to see the lives of the poor, already difficult, made even harder

- I don't want to see American children in masks (few countries are doing this) and I certainly don't want to see their parents bullied into subjecting them to an experimental medical procedure that has zero medical justification

Thus my alliance with Robert F. Kennedy, Jr. which started April 19, 2021.

At some point, I'll document all the things I've done behind the scenes to get this book to #1 on Amazon. It's a nice accomplishment, but here's a pro's tip: It's just the warm-up for the real work to come.

Meanwhile, I have been and will continue to be sharing the "play-by-play" with my System Club members, the only folks who've had access to me and what I'm up to since 2011.

Oh, and get the book today. Better yet, buy ten. (https://www.amazon.com/Real-Anthony-Fauci-Democracy-Childrens/dp/1510766804)

Called it, did it – Episode 2

November 24, 2021

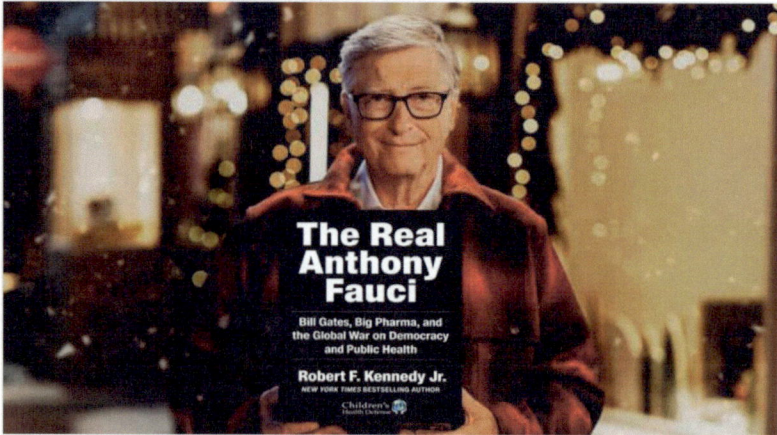

Readers of this blog know that I've been on Fauci's trail since March of 2020, and writing about it in detail since June of that year (https://KenMcCarthy.com/blog/who-the-hell-is-tony-fauci-and-why-did-we-annihilate-the-world-economy-based-on-his-say-so).

My System Club members know that I contributed research to Robert F. Kennedy Jr.'s book (see acknowledgment in the book, page xii, second paragraph) and that in October I got heavily involved in advising the promotional campaign.

When I started, the book was #153 and I told the Kennedy people we could get it to #1 and I laid out exactly what needed to be done to achieve it. They did most of the important things, all of which were a revelation to them (though ABC stuff for my students.)

Last week, I said that to be on the Amazon bestsellers list for one day is meaningless. We're going for ownership of the top slots through Thanksgiving – at least.

As of this moment (6:40 PM, November 24, the day before Thanksgiving) – more than a week after the launch – we're #1 hardcover, #1 Kindle and #3 on audiobooks. (They didn't fully follow my advice on audio, though I did get them from #80 to Top 3. What can I say?)

How did we do it?

Wouldn't you like to know.

System Club members know.

Right now, we're waiting to hear on the New York Times bestseller list.

If we get it and we should, that's good. If we don't, it means we've been unfairly excluded and we have our next media campaign.

Heads we win. Tails we win.

This just in: 6:55 PM The Real Anthony Fauci is #7 on the New York Times bestsellers list. Let the games begin.

Stay tuned. We're now almost properly warmed up.

Oh, and get the book today. Better yet, buy ten. (https://www.amazon.com/Real-Anthony-Fauci-Democracy-Childrens/dp/1510766804/)

Chapter 4

The First Meaningful Act of Push Back

Rally to stop forced vaccination of children and others

December 30, 2021

Wednesday, January 5

As New York goes, so goes the rest of the country.

As is typical of New York, they're creating unhinged rules to "regulate" COVID that if applied to the rest of the country will be a nationwide disaster.

Do you live in New York State or any of its adjacent states (Vermont, Connecticut, Massachusetts, New Jersey, Pennsylvania)?

Do you have friends, family or colleagues in these states?

Please share this important message with them and encourage them to share it widely.

It's essential that medical authoritarianism based on fraud, and all the proposed legislation related to it, be shut down and we can do it if we show up in force in January.

Please click here, download the flyer, and post it widely in your community.

(https://KenMcCarthy.com/blog/wp-
content/uploads/2021/12/tfc_bw_flyer_12.28.21v2.pdf)

If everyone takes care of their corner of the world –
library, supermarket, post office, public bulletin boards, light
polls – we could saturate the relevant region with this
message.

God Bless Canada – Pass it on

January 29, 2022

I've loved Canada since I took my first trip there as a little kid when my family took a vacation to Expo in Montreal, Quebec.

One of my distant ancestors Gaelic-speaking Florence McCarthy, came to the U.S. (Oswego, NY) via Canada from Ireland.

Some of my best friends are Canadians and I've had some of the biggest fun of my life there.

I even angled to get my wife Canadian citizenship. Her Dad was born there and it worked.

Of course, in our world, the pioneering work of two Canadians, Corey Rudl and Michael Campbell, is about as central to Internet marketing as can be.

Thus the horror and sadness I've felt watching my friends and other Canadians so roundly abused by what can only be called a criminal regime.

And who is attempting to come to the rescue?

Real people who actually work for a living.

Clarification: To the morons who think I'm a fan of FOX, I've probably published more words against FOX and

Rupert Murdoch than you have published cumulatively in your entire life. They, for some reason, happen to be the only people reporting the news on this story so I have to go with what I've got.

One cautionary note: The former Chief of Toronto Police, Bill Blair, under whose management the most egregious violations of civil rights occurred in Canada in modern times, is now Canada's Minister of Emergency Preparedness. If there is an "incident", be aware that he and the people he works for are capable of anything.

Go Canada!

February 03, 2022

The garbage news media in Canada is telling people that the demonstrators are racist, misogynist, and violent.

The garbage news media in the U.S. (and elsewhere) is not reporting the size of the protests. It's MILLIONS of people on their feet and in the streets in a country of just 38 million.

For a profession that lies for a living (the news media), they are outdoing themselves.

Spread the word among your friends, neighbors and – if you have any balls – your customers and clients.

Canadians are showing us the way out.

If we don't take it, the everlasting shame is on us.

Reasons to be cheerful – and a warning

February 09, 2022

I'd love nothing more than to devote all my energy to preparing for the 20th anniversary of the System Seminar.

But given a choice, I'd rather celebrate the liberation of the people of Canada and all the other people around the world whose fates depend on the courage, good will and intelligence of their example.

Canadian "authorities" have been taking food, water, and fuel from truckers in Ottawa, in an attempt to starve and freeze them out. The citizens of Ottawa have retaliated in humorous, peaceful ways.

Now I'm going to ask a hard question.

Canadians love their children and grandchildren.

Why don't we?

Suicide attempts by teenaged girls are up 51% during the illegal lockdowns and bogus emergency decrees. How much clearer an indication of the suffering this madness has inflicted on our children do we need before we take action?

I'm sorry to say I see the vast majority of my profession sitting on their hands doing and saying nothing. I hope that will change – and soon.

I want to commend Dave Farr, System grad, who has devoted many hundreds of hours using his marketing, communications and organizational skills to help hold it down in Minnesota on behalf of his fellow citizens there. This is their group: Masks Off Minnesota (https://maskoffmn.org/).

We know the vaccines don't work (specifically don't stop infection or spread)... we know children are not and have never been at risk... we know the make-believe masks are a sinister joke... and we know children are suffering real harm from the masks, the insane measures being taken by the schools, and now the vaccines which the CDC/FDA's own VAERS database documents is generating injury reports at a rate greater than any other vaccine in history.

What's it going to take for us to say no to this monstrosity?

Thank to the Canadians for shaking things loose (Lorne Michaels is a Canadian)

March 03, 2022

[VIDEO AT https://KenMcCarthy.com/blog/a-fresh-breeze-from-canada]

Google/YouTube doesn't want you to see this but somehow it made it onto network TV.

The 100-foot steel wall of lies and censorship is starting to shake.

First, the Robert F. Kennedy Jr. book exposing Fauci's frauds, which recently crossed the 1 million copies sold mark.

Then, the frankly miraculous coming together of the free people of Canada.

Now, this "green light" from on high to comedians that it's now "acceptable" to mock and ridicule this vicious and sinister two-year fraud.

Comedy in general and Saturday Night Live, in particular, are VERY powerful cultural and subversive forces which can be – and often are – consciously used for good and evil.

Saturday Night Live looks like they're finally getting it right.

Is it a "coincidence" that a Canadian runs the show?

Lorne Michaels – creator and producer of Saturday Night Live – is Canadian.

Other Canadians on Saturday Night Live over the years.

Ottawa-born Dan Aykroyd (1975-79)

Peter Aykroyd (1979-80), Brantford

Ontario's Phil Hartman (1986-94)

Quebec City's Norm Macdonald (1993-98)

Ottawa-born Mark McKinney (1995-97)

Toronto's Mike Myers (1989-95)

Hamilton, Ontario native Martin Short (1984-85)

Just for fun, some other Canadian comedians:

Jim Carrey

Tom Green

John Candy

Seth Rogan

Leslie Nielsen

Eugene Levy

Tommy Chong

Paul Shaffer

With less than 10% of the size of the US population, Canada punches way above its weight in comedy.

There's power in humor and while Canada doesn't have nuclear weapons, its funny bone makes it a very formidable force in the world.

You should know what happened in Canada

March 07, 2022

[VIDEO AT - https://KenMcCarthy.com/blog/you-should-know-what-happened-in-canada]

An informative and heart warming film about how the beautiful and courageous people of Canada showed the world how to stand up to government insanity, corruption and tyranny.

If you've depended on the news media and/or have not had hours to research the citizenship journalism that made its way past the censors on the Internet, you missed one of the greatest shows on earth.

Made by yours truly with the help of Paul Morrison, a recent grad of the Advanced Info Marketing and Copywriting Program.

1,000,000 hardcover copies sold

March 20, 2022

Ken with Tony Lyons, president of Skyhorse Publishing.

On November 6, I encouraged you to get a copy (or copies) of Robert F. Kennedy Jr.'s new book "The Real Anthony Fauci."

As people who follow the blog know, I've been dogging Fauci since March of 2020.

When I heard Robert Kennedy Jr. was working on a book on Fauci, I contributed my research files to the effort (a video I made, "Fauci's First Fraud" is cited 25 times in the book - https://www.youtube.com/watch?v=wy3frBacd2k)

I also rolled up my sleeves and helped with the marketing.

That's me on the right and Tony Lyons, owner of Skyhorse Publishing, the book's publisher, on the left.

Despite being deliberately ignored by the news media – no reviews, no articles, only a few media interviews, and a boycott by many "woke" bookstores – the book passed an important milestone recently: 1,000,000 hardcover copies sold.

How did we do it?

I gave the blow-by-blow account as it was happening to members of my System Club. (The recordings are in the System Club archive)

Selling over 1,000,000 hardcover copies of a book in less than five months with zero news media support is not something that happens every day.

Now we're plotting how to sell the second million. System Club (https://www.thesystemclub.com/private) members will get the inside story as it unfolds.

Now it's time to round up the bad guys and help those who were harmed

April 20, 2022

Starting in March 2020 I began educating people about the following facts:

1. Fauci is a fraud, a liar, an incompetent, and a con artist and anyone following his guidance on medical or public health matters is going to wake up with a very bad hangover.

2. The CoVid Hysteria was and is a media campaign to sell vaccines – beginning, middle, and end of the story.

3. We have been down this same road before and eventually people are going to wake up.

"Why not wake up now," I asked. "BEFORE countless millions of people are needlessly harmed?"

Well, I did my bit and I'm sorry to say many "gurus" either sat on their hands and said nothing or worse actually contributed labor, free, and in some cases paid (see infomercial producer Steve Dworman's work for the LA School District), to promote the unhinged cause.

The people who did this to you

The CoVid Con was – and is – a MASSIVE payday for many people…

The vaccine makers, of course…

The mask makers…

The test-people-every-day-forever makers…

The consultants…

The box stores and chain restaurants that thrived while small businesses were forcibly shut down…

The hospitals that got bonuses for declaring "CoVid cases" even among people who were already fatally sick with other ailments…

The local idiot politicians who were given a pretense for being on TV every day appearing to be important (as well as a new source of kickbacks as they parceled out federal CoVid money that flowed without limit.)…

Even drug dealers and liquor stores profited and we know that from the catastrophic explosion in suicides, fatal overdoses, and deaths from alcohol that the con triggered.

Then there were the ad people… the PR people… the social psychologists… the government spokespeople… the news media liars… and others who were paid to distort the science and cook up an endless variety of ways to scare the public out of their minds so they'd comply with every dictate no matter how ludicrous and socially destructive.

What this was all about and what needs to happen next?

The whole thing was a big marketing campaign crafted by sinister people and executed by legions of idiots, cowards, and outright crooks.

Yes, some people died with CoVid. Vulnerable people die every year from all sorts of things including colds and flu but we don't throw millions of people into poverty and despair, interrupt the education and development of children, or destroy tens of thousands of family businesses over it.

But from 2020 to 2022 we did.

The masks didn't work. (The pre-2020 science told us they wouldn't.) The "safe and effective" vaccines have proven to be neither. Double vaccinated and boosted people catch and spread CoVid.

VAERS (Vaccine Adverse Reaction Reporting System), the joint FDA/CDC vaccine injury statistics reporting service, shows CoVid vaccines have caused more injuries than all other vaccines administered over the last 40 years combined, in what may end up being the worse self-administered public health catastrophe in history. And there are still idiots demanding that people get vaccinated and boosted or lose their jobs, their access to services and even to society.

It's time to stop – and hunt down the evildoers behind this thing and prosecute and hopefully imprison them for what they did.

Two years late, but better late than never

May 14, 2022

The science is in.

The early fatality rate projections were a fraud.

Mask-wearing as a safety measure was a fraud.

The deliberate blocking of a wide range of early intervention therapies was a fraud – and a homicidal one at that.

The socially catastrophic lockdowns made no difference whatsoever to the public health outcome other than to increase human misery to the point of never-before-seen levels of suicide, death from alcoholism, and drug overdose, not to mention the forcing of at least 150 million of the world's already-struggling into extreme poverty.

The rushed-by-fraud-and-hysteria vaccines, based on speculative, garbage science, are not effective.

The vaccines are proving to be dangerous and are already known to be doing more incontrovertible, measurable harm to certain populations (like boys and young men) than CoVid has.

It still mystifies me how all this was not seen as a highly likely outcome of this non-stop fraud fest.

There was never any science or logic or reason behind any of it, just world-class propaganda, bullshit, corruption, and cowardice.

Extraordinary claims were made not only without extraordinary proof but also, in many cases, with fraudulent evidence.

Thousands of years of basic common sense about health and medical experience were thrown out of the window and replaced with literal insanity (example: quarantining the healthy.)

This was, as I said in March of 2020, a vaccine marketing exercise, and shame on any "marketing expert" who took months and even years to see it. (As of this writing, some still haven't.)

I can see people being fooled in the early days, even the early months, but to actively promote the vaccines as some have? Mind-boggling.

So what's next?

A sane society would document, track down, and record every criminal and idiot who promoted this thing.

Thanks to the magic of the Internet, every comment made during this fraud was dated and time-stamped.

I note that recently some people are starting to scrub their social media. This includes one very high-profile doctor in NYC who lied shamelessly non-stop about the risk of CoVid to children and now has gone so far as to delete her entire Twitter channel.

As of this moment, we see that the people most responsible for this – government at all levels, the news media, the criminally negligent medical profession, and its pharma overlords – are doing everything they can to stamp out information, conversation, and truth-telling, calling it "disinformation."

They're angling to make themselves the ultimate arbiters of what can and cannot be discussed, even when they've been caught in so many blatant lies the past two years they're virtually uncountable.

We'll see how that works out for them.

The arc of history is long and truth has an inconvenient way of ultimately finding its way to the surface.

Meanwhile, expect the equivalent of a World War III effort on the part of the people responsible for this to suppress information and public conversation about their crimes.

The next book we have to get behind

June 12, 2022

If you've been following the blog since April 2021, you know I contributed to the Robert F. Kennedy Jr book, sending him content that first appeared on this site starting in March 2020.

My film "Fauci's First Fraud," which I assembled from over 40 years of archival footage of Faucis career, is cited in the book twenty-five times.

I also rolled up my sleeves in October and directed key elements of the book's launch and promotion in the first two month afterwards. (Over 1 million hard covers sold in the face of a near-total news media blackout.)

This is the next book we need to get behind: **"The Bodies of Others: The New Authoritarians, COVID-19 and The War Against the Human"**

Naomi Wolf nails it comprehensively – with references and in clear and compelling language.

This is the book I would have written if I'd had the time.

In fact, readers following my commentary on the CoVid Con since March of 2020 will recognize many of the facts and anecdotes presented in this excellent book. The facts were available to all who cared to research or at least follow the research of others.

The CoVid Con was and is not just a "confederacy of dunces" of idiot local politicians, cowardly doctors and public health careerists, and a moronic and easily corrupted news media.

The CoVid Con was a very well thought out, meticulously planned, and brilliantly executed attack on human life as we know it, and was carried out on behalf of an alliance of people who saw a profit in it for themselves and indeed did profit massively from it - namely Pharma, Big Tech, corporate giants like Amazon, and the easily-corruptible and irresponsible news industry.

Every essential element of normal human life – family, community, contact with others, live music, religion, education – was systematically undermined using clearly fabricated scientific and medical justification while the beneficiaries – virtual media, dangerous medical treatments, big box stores, corporate restaurant chains, and even drug dealers – saw their profits boosted to unprecedented levels.

Many people reading this already understand all this.

Many, inexplicably, still do not.

Wolf makes it crystal clear in book form like no one else has.

Get the book, talk about the book, get copies for friends and family, and for local libraries.

A great deal is at stake here.

"The Bodies of Others: The New Authoritarians, COVID-19 and The War Against the Human"

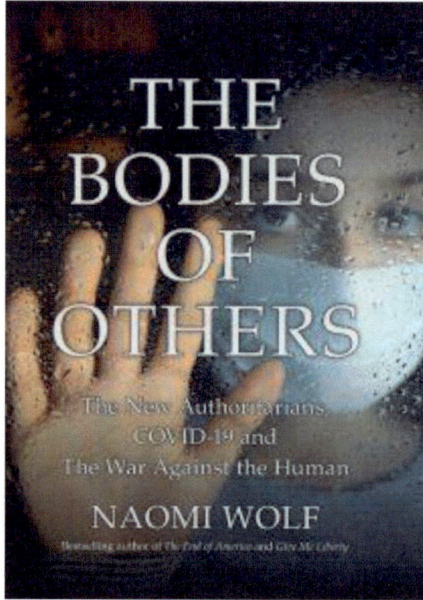

They're finally catching up with what we knew in March 2020 – two years ago if you're counting

June 16, 2022

Vinay Prasad is an MD and an MPH. He's also a practicing physician in the field of hematology-oncology as well as an Associate Professor of Epidemiology and Biostatistics at the University of California San Francisco.

He has his own lab at the university which studies cancer drug development, the quality of medical evidence, clinical trial design, health care policy, and better medical decision making.

In other words, his opinion is somewhat more informed than that of county public health officials, hospital administrators, governors with political science degrees, and blow-dried talking head idiots on TV – in other words, the people who have been controlling health, economic, and human rights policy for the world the last two years.

Though he's a Kool-Aid drinker on the subjects of Vaccination Inc. and Cancer Inc., two of the most disreputable industries in medicine if not on earth, he knows bullshit when he sees it and, now that the coast is getting clear, he's becoming more and more outspoken.

Interestingly, YouTube hasn't removed his videos, demonetized them, or erased his account as they have done to so many doctors and scientists. Maybe the censors at YouTube lack subtlety, because he's essentially calling the CoVid Hysteria, and all that came along with it, a medical fraud without any scientific justification whatsoever.

...Just like we've been saying since the lockdowns started.

The masks were a fraud from Day One

June 17, 2022

I've been saying this for two years now and it's based on well established science that's over 70 years old that was EASILY discoverable for anyone who cared to look.

Most countries where the leaders have a brain cell between them NEVER masked children, but in the US children have been masked continuously and in some places it's still going on!

There's no justification for it - THERE NEVER WAS - and unlike Fauci's BS science, the injuries these masks are causing children and others is measurable. This particular madness has got to stop.

And don't get me started on the criminality of approving a still inadequately tested medical intervention on INFANTS who don't have any need for it.

Time for people to man and woman up and start protecting children.

I first pointed this out here on July 20, 2020, but some people didn't get the memo.

I knew this because there's something called industrial hygiene and people in that field have been studying the mask issue for over 70 years.

Not only don't masks work for CoVid-sized viral particles, they are well known to be dangerous to the health of fully developed adults - which I guess is why some schools, libraries, local governments, airlines etc. insisted that small children wear them.

Anyone who put a child on a mask without doing their homework is guilty of child abuse. Period. That "the government made me do it" is not an answer.

The doctors who went along with this and told their patients it was real should have their licenses pulled. They're dangerous idiots.

Don't believe me?

Here's a graphic from Stephen Petty (B.S.Ch.E., M.S.Ch.E., M.B.A.) Unlike the morons who've been pushing masks, Petty is a Certified Industrial Hygienist, and a Certified Safety Professional, and a professional engineer in addition to all his other degrees. A little more informed about the matter than your local public health idiot.

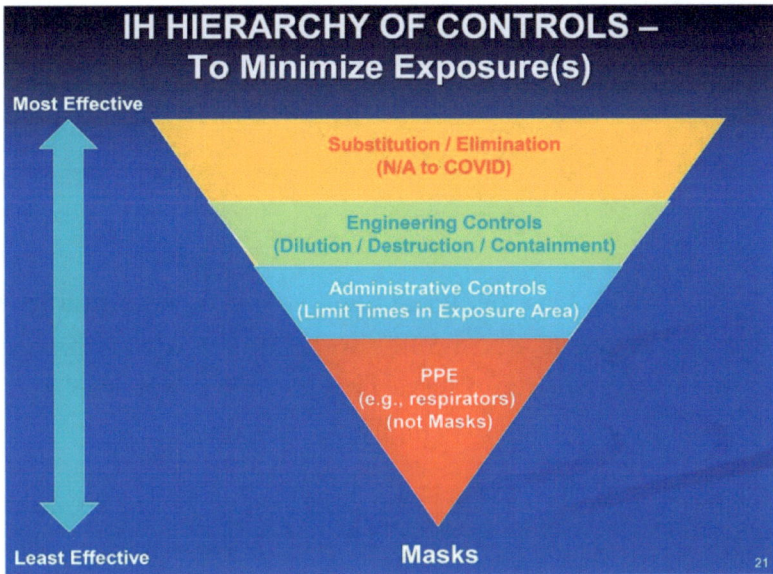

Industrial Hygiene Hierarchy of Controls. Masks, dead last.

Sinister beyond belief

June 26, 2022

The FDA has declared that it's now acceptable for children as young as six months to be injected with products we know don't work and have proven to be injurious and in some cases deadly to many, many thousands.

No other country in the world is engaged in similar madness.

Fortunately, as of now, most parents are not going for it and the deranged politicians showing up at these hot shot vaccination assembly lines for photo ops are being disappointed.

Good, but how far are we from these psychopaths mandating this experimental gene therapy (Moderna's own description of its product) for newborns, for daycare, for Kindergarten, for primary school?

This has been the game since Day One: Maneuver children into receiving a lifetime of mRNA shots.

I'm sorry to see, with the overturning of Roe v. Wade, adult women losing federal legal protection for their right to make their own health decisions regarding pregnancy.

That said I'm appalled that many of the same women who are making the most noise about that problem helped promote, or least quietly tolerated, two year olds being forced to wear masks all day in daycare, young people blocked from a college education unless they agree to be unpaid subjects in medical experiments, and tens of thousands of nurses and firemen who lost their jobs for refusing a medical procedure that has been proven to be ineffective and unsafe.

Where have these champions of freedom been the last two plus years?

On the one hand, we have a medical option made more difficult. On the other, we have people being compelled to take injections, likely multiple injections, of products we know not only do not work as advertised but are also clearly proving to be downright dangerous.

If you have managed to remain ignorant on this last point, the rushed, unproven, and inadequately tested CoVid vaccines have, according to the U.S. government's own database, killed and injured more people than all previous injectable vaccines combined over the last thirty-two years. Go here for details - https://openvaers.com/

Two rebellious Irishmen kicking ass on behalf of humanity. Ken (right) with Robert F. Kennedy Jr. (left)

SABATEAN FRANKISTS.

GEORGIA GUIDE STONES

KHAZAR - KHAZARIAN (SILK ROAD)

TALMUDISTS

THE NAME STEALERS.

Manufactured by Amazon.ca
Bolton, ON